JUDO a pictorial manual

Keiko Fukuda Sensei (7th dan) throwing Pat Harrington. Fukuda Sensei's Australian Tour, July 1965.

JUDO a pictorial manual

Pat Harrington

Photographs by Betty Huxley

Charles E. Tuttle Company
Rutland, Vermont & Tokyo, Japan

Miss Pat Harrington and Miss Sandra McCuish demonstrating *Goshin-ho*, Forms of Women's Self Defence.

Published by the Charles E. Tuttle Company, Inc.
of Rutland, Vermont & Tokyo, Japan
with editorial offices at
2-6 Suido 1-chome, Bunkyo-ku, Tokyo 112
© 1987 by Pat Harrington (text) and Betty Huxley (photographs)

© 1992 by Charles E. Tuttle Publishing Co., Inc.

First Tuttle edition, 1992
Second printing, 1993

LCC Card No. 92-60338
ISBN 0-8048-1878-9

Printed in Japan

Contents

6

Foreword

I have great pleasure in knowing that Judo which originated from the martial art of Ju-jitsu and developed to the physical training of Judo is now an international sport and will be played in the Tokyo Olympics of 1964.

Ju-jitsu gained its origin during the age of the civil war when Samurais grappled with each other wearing armour suits and then developed in the Tokugawa Era as Ju-jitsu and many styles were developed.

In the Meiji Era, 39th year of July, 1905, when the martial arts association held its meeting in Kyoto city of Japan, the director of the Kodokan Judo Institute, Jigoro Kano and other directors of each style of Ju-jitsu gathered together and decided upon Judo forms of physical training from Ju-jitsu. These forms are still being taught to this present day.

On the other hand Ju-jitsu was considered to be the past ancient Martial Art which was superseded by Judo, but each school still has its own style which has been handed down throughout generation to generation of family inheritance. Sosuishiryu which has been handed down to my dojo 'Sekiryu-kan' is one of the few remaining schools of Ju-jitsu.

I believe it is really valuable for Miss Patricia Harrington who visited my dojo at this time to have studied these forms and experienced and understood this type of Japanese Martial Art.

Originally the word 'Martial Art' meant an art developed for protecting oneself from attack. If one masters this art successfully one will always be able to prevent harm being inflicted. Unfortunately if you are attacked by an opponent, but are preparing for this attack by having a peaceful mind and a body well trained, you will no longer desire to fight with people. You will be at peace with the world.

It is most important for the Martial Arts, not only to practice its forms, but also to practice control and unity of mind and body. One who persists in being aggressive is indeed a failure as a student and should be ashamed of oneself.

Miss Harrington has studied the Japanese Martial Arts for many years and her endeavour is admirable.

In conclusion I wish to express my admiration and respect from the bottom of my heart for her

publication *Judo, a Pictorial Manual* and pray for her success.

August 10, 1964

Shusaku Shitama,
15th Inheritor of Sosuishiryu Ju-jutsu

Shusaku (Shuzo) Shitama, past President of the Nippon Sosuishiryu Kai, (The Sosuishiryu Martial Arts Association of Japan) who was the Master Instructor (10th dan, Dai Shihan) of the Sekiryukan, Headquarters of the Sosuishiryu Academy in Fukuoka, Japan. Master Shitama was the 15th Inheritor of the organisation and succeeded Kibei Aoyagi in 1925. He graduated from the Judo Department of the Butokukai Martial Arts Academy in Kyoto and held the rank of 8th dan in Kodokan judo and was the President of the Fukuoka prefecture of the Kodokan Judo Institute. Shusaku Shitama died on 30 June 1966 in his mid fifties.

Acknowledgements

I would like to thank Mr Michael John Huxley for many long and arduous hours spent developing and printing the 1134 photographs in this book. Michael Huxley donated his time and special skills in the name of friendship and such friends are rare gems indeed.

I wish to express my special thanks and appreciation to Sensei Ichiro Abe, Director of the International Affairs Division of the Kodokan Judo Institute and Sensei Haruko Niboshi, Chief Instructress of the Women's Division (Joshi Bu) of the Kodokan Judo Institute for taking time from their already over-crammed schedules to correct the techniques and terminology in this book.

I would like to thank Sensei Naoka Miyajima, of the Women's Division (Joshi Bu) of the Kodokan Judo Institute for the amount of hard work and patience she contributed to the translation of *History of Women's Judo in the World* by Sanzo Maruyama.

I wish to thank Miss Sandra McCuish, Sandan (Kodokan), for the amount of hard work contributed as my demonstration partner throughout this book.

Special thanks to Mr Terry Jones of Century-graphics for the front cover artwork.

I would like to thank Mr Neil Manns for the photograph on the front cover and the photographs on pages 84 and 85.

In conclusion, I would like to thank the following students who assisted me in the photographs for squad training:

Mr Neil Manns, Nidan
Mr Ron Mason, Nidan
Miss Ann Lloyd, Nidan
Miss Dianne Coote, Shodan
Miss Claudia Fabreski, Shodan
Mr Barry Windeatt, Shodan
Miss Cassandra Daw

Special thanks to Mrs Shirley Wall, née Harrington, for the drawings on page 182 of variation *Harai-goshi*.

I wish to express my sincere gratitude to Mrs Betty Huxley for the excellence of her photographic contribution to this judo manual.

I feel that, to photograph judo techniques, one has to be a judoka to know the right moment to click the camera. Betty has taken each technique at the crucial split second necessary to illustrate explicitly each step.

In addition to all this, Betty has spent many long hours sorting, correlating and cropping each photograph as each batch came out of the dark-room, a task which turned out to be the most exhausting of all in the production of this manual.

Betty Huxley

| Pat Harrington | Kitaoka Sensei | H. Niboshi Sensei | N. Miyajima Sensei | B. Huxley |
| 5th dan | 5th dan | 7th dan | 5th dan | 4th dan |

| Pat Harrington | Betty Huxley | Sandra McCuish |
| 5th dan | 4th dan | 3rd dan |

At the Kodokan Judo Institute, Women's Division (*Joshi Bu*), December 1975.

I wish to dedicate this judo manual to my judo instructors (Sensei), both past and present.

Teachers are the vessels through which God's knowledge is conveyed and I am extremely grateful for the knowledge which I have received.

The late Kyuzo Mifune Sensei (10th dan) and Pat Harrington at the Kodokan Judo Institute (International Headquarters of Judo), August 1964. Mifune Sensei died on 27 January 1965.

Keiko Fukuda Sensei and Pat Harrington. Fukuda Sensei's Australian Tour, July 1965.

Introduction

It has long been my strongest wish to write a complete judo manual. During my years as a judo student, I could not find a judo manual which contained all of the techniques and katas which I was required to learn. Furthermore, I could not find an instructor in Australia, at that time, who could teach me all of the requirements. This situation made me make the important decision to save up and visit the Kodokan Judo Institute in Japan, and I have been returning there as often as possible ever since.

I then realised that there must be thousands of judo students all over the world who are in the same predicament, but who cannot afford to visit Japan, and for this reason I have attempted to write a complete judo manual with all of the technical and kata requirements up to Yondan or 4th degree black belt.

I have felt for a long time that there is too much emphasis placed upon the shiai or contest aspect of judo today and not enough attention given to the technical, kata, mental and spiritual aspects of judo. There are twelve aspects of judo, and a judoka should faithfully practise all aspects regularly, without neglecting any of them, in order to correctly develop and fully mature one's attitude towards judo.

Judo, as Jigoro Kano founded,
   is based on the principles he expounded.
Faithful practice throughout a judoka's life,
   will advance one spiritually and enhance
      one's life.

Pat Harrington

(Left) Dr Kano (Above) Dr Kano's handwriting
'Mutual Welfare & Benefit, Maximum-Efficiency'

JIGORO KANO

History of Judo

The Origin of Judo

The originator of judo, Professor Jigoro Kano was born on 28 October 1860, in the seaside town of Mikage, near Kobe, Japan. He moved with his family to Tokyo in 1871.

This was a difficult time in Japanese history as the Tokugawa Shogunate had disintegrated and

Imperial rule had been restored (Meiji Restoration) in 1868. The ordinance of 1871 prohibiting Samurai from wearing swords caused a rapid decline in all martial arts. Various *ju jutsu* schools, which were strongly established in a great many clan capitals, began to diminish. When Jigoro Kano reached the age of eighteen years, he became interested in learning *ju jutsu*. He was never exceptionally strong, nor did he have a big physique, but he realised that *ju jutsu* was an art

On 24 July 1905, representatives of the leading Ju jutsu schools (Ryus) of Japan, gathered at the Butokukai Institute in Kyoto to agree upon the forms of Kodokan Judo and to continue the development of the technical forms of the sport. The ancient Ju jutsu techniques of each particular school were to be preserved in *kata* (pre-arranged form) for posterity.

which stressed the correct use of energy regardless of one's strength or physique and, as a student of Tokyo Imperial University, he began to search for a suitable teacher. His first teacher was Teinosuke Yagi, Sensei. He later studied under Hachinosuke Fukuda Sensei, grandfather of Keiko Fukuda Sensei, and Masatomo Iso Sensei of the Tenshin Shinyo Ryu, and Tsunetoshi Iikubo Sensei of the Kito Ryu, and was initiated into the secret teachings of both schools.

With typical enthusiasm, Jigoro Kano continued to explore the mysteries of other schools as well as to improve his own system. He made many visits to other famous teachers (*sensei*) of *ju jutsu* and also to study the old *densho*, the manuscript records of secrets developed by the founders of various schools. He also studied the *I Ching*, (Book of Changes) and the philosophy of the very famous Chinese philosopher, Lao-Tsze.

Because of the revolutionary changes in Japanese history at this particular time, it was inevitable that ancient *ju jutsu* principles, formerly taught for highly practical purposes in feudal warfare, were about to be re-established in principle and purpose and propagated far and wide.

In 1882, Jigoro Kano founded the Kodokan Judo Institute in Tokyo, Japan. *Ko* means 'lecture' or 'practice', *do* means 'way', and *kan* means 'hall'. The original Kodokan hall was only twelve tatami mats in size and was situated in the Eisho temple in the Shitaya district of Tokyo. In this first dojo (practice hall), Jigoro Kano began teaching his own system, which he renamed *judo*. The word judo is derived from two syllables, *ju*, meaning 'gentle' or 'pliable', and *do*, meaning 'way'. With this new system, based upon the principle of pliability of mind and body, nonresistance to opposing strength, the best use of energy, judo began to grow and become enormously popular. The formula of Kodokan Judo was completed about 1887. The Kodokan Judo Institute had three broad aims: physical education, contest proficiency and mental training. As well as being a fighting art, judo is a sport and a form of physical and mental training based on scientific principles; a 'way' of human development that can be understood by people all over the world.

In 1889, Jigoro Kano visited Europe and the United States of America for the first time and thereafter he travelled abroad a total of eight times to teach judo. His leading disciples made a great contribution to the development of judo in the world and, often in the face of extreme hardship, they devoted their lives to planting the seed of judo in foreign countries.

The famous mottos of Kodokan Judo were such slogans as *Seriyoku-zenyo* (maximum efficiency) and *Jita-kyoei* (mutual welfare and benefit). Kodokan judo was virtually made safe enough for people of all ages to practise, unlike the former art, *ju jutsu*. Children could commence training at the age of nine years and continue until ninety years old, if so desired. The Kodokan Judo Institute was open for enrolment for people from all walks of life, without exception. Great emphasis was placed upon the correct moral and spiritual training. The ultimate goal was to strive enthusiastically for self-perfection as a human being. In 1900, the Kodokan Dan Grade Holders Association was established. The spiritual phase was gradually developed and was completed around 1922. In the same year the Kodokan Cultural Judo Society was established.

From the technical standpoint, Jigoro Kano began by taking the *atemi-waza* (striking points) and *katame-waza* (grappling techniques) of the Tenjin Shinyo School and the *nage-waza* (throwing syllabus) of the Kito School. The techniques which complied with scientific principles were retained, and others were rejected. Then new techniques were added and the result was a system designed to meet the requirements of those days. The system was a combination of intellectual and moral education, as well as a method of combat.

In 1909, the system underwent a big change and the Kodokan became a foundation. In the same year Jigoro Kano became the first Japanese member of the International Olympic Committee and two years later he founded the Japanese Athletic Association and became its first president. In the months that followed he established the Kodokan Judo Instructors' Training Department. Beginning with the fifth Olympiad in Stockholm, he attended every Olympic Games and International Olympic Committee meeting and became a leading figure in international sport. At the meeting of the International Olympic Committee held in Cairo in 1938, Jigoro Kano succeeded in having Tokyo approved as the venue for the twelfth Olympiad. On his way home to Japan from Cairo, Jigoro Kano became ill and died of pneumonia aboard the s.s. *Hikawa Maru* on 4 May 1938, at the age of seventy-eight years.

As an educator, Professor Jigoro Kano graduated in 1881 at the age of twenty-two years from the Tokyo Imperial University. He became Professor at the Gakushuin (Peers' school) in Tokyo. In 1889 he toured educational institutions in Europe, gaining an insight into educational systems overseas. In 1891 he became a Councillor of the Education Ministry. In 1893 he was appointed head of the library section of the Education Ministry. He was then appointed headmaster of the First National High School and later, in the same year, headmaster of the Tokyo Teachers' Training School. In 1898, he was appointed Head of General School Affairs with the Department of the Ministry of Education. In 1902, he established a school for exchange students from China. In 1924, he was appointed Emeritus Professor of the Tokyo Teachers' Training School.

As a sportsman and a physical educator, Jigoro Kano originated the sport of judo from the ancient principles of *ju jutsu* and developed the technical and spiritual aspects of the sport to the highest possible level. He contributed enormously to the propagation of judo throughout the world and its inclusion as an Olympic sport. In his lifetime, he attained a doctorate degree in judo, a degree equivalent to the twelfth dan, awarded to the originator of judo only. He also founded the Japan Athletic Association in 1911, and was constantly working to produce physical education instructors to ensure the rapid development of athletics and Japanese sport in general. He can indeed be called the father of physical education and sport in Japan. In 1935, he was awarded the Asahi prize for his outstanding contribution to the organising of sport in Japan during his lifetime.

All this is expressed in the following words, which were Kano Shihan's legacy:

Judo is a means of using mental and physical energy most effectively. This training means improving oneself physically and spiritually through the practice of self-defence techniques and learning through experience the essence of the 'way'. This, then, is the ultimate object of judo—to perfect oneself and thus be of some use to the world around.

Expansion of Judo

In 1889, Jigoro Kano toured Europe and America. His leading disciples did a great deal to propagate Kodokan judo overseas. Jigoro Kano made as many as eight trips abroad to teach and spread the principles of Kodokan judo.

One of the first foreign dignitaries to study judo at the Kodokan under Professor Yamashita in 1904 was Theodore Roosevelt, President of the United States of America at that time. Even before 1912 people from England, the United States of America, Korea, China, India, France and Canada took lessons in judo at the Kodokan.

Mr Gunji Koizumi, 7th dan, founder of judo in Great Britain, also founded the Budokwai in London in 1918. He later founded the British Judo Association. His contribution to judo was enormous and he has written text books of judo to serve as a technical guide to his students.

Mikinosuke Kawaishi, 7th dan, founder of judo in France, also made valuable contributions in his lifetime to the development of judo, publishing several judo and self-defence manuals.

Around 1922, judo associations were established in France, Brazil and the United States of America. In 1948, the British Judo Association and the European Judo Federation were established in London. In 1949, the All Japan Judo Federation was founded.

After the Second World War, occupation forces, mainly consisting of American G.I. soldiers and officers, became extremely proficient in the Japanese martial arts, in particular Kodokan judo, and as a result the Armed Forces Judo Association of U.S.A. was established. These servicemen and women took a wealth of knowledge back to America when they eventually returned to their homeland.

In 1951, Risei Kano, son of the founder of judo and president of the Kodokan Judo Institute from

1946 until 1979, made a goodwill tour with several of the most prominent Kodokan masters throughout Europe and America.

In 1952, on the seventieth anniversary of the Kodokan Judo Institute, the International Judo Federation was founded and Risei Kano was its first president. In 1955, Risei Kano dispatched a team of judo teachers (*sensei*) and judo students overseas to further the progress of Kodokan judo.

In 1956, the first world championships, for men only, were held in Tokyo. In 1958, the new Kodokan building, built at 1–16, Kasuga-cho, Bunkyo-ku, Tokyo, was completed and became the headquarters of the International Judo Federation. On 2 November 1958, the second world championships for men were held. In 1964, judo was included for the first time, for men only, in the Olympic Games held in Tokyo. In 1965, Mr Charles Palmer of England became president of the International Judo Federation and remained so for a period of fourteen years until, in December 1979, Mr Shigeyoshi Matsumae became the new president. Mr Shigeyoshi Matsumae is also president of the Nippon Budokan and of the Japanese Budo Association.

In 1979, Risei Kano retired as president of the Kodokan Judo Institute and his son, Mr Yukimitsu Kano, became the new president.

In 1980, almost one hundred years since the inception of Kodokan judo, women were represented in the first world championships for women, held in Maddison Square Gardens, New York. This event took place twenty-four years after the first world championships for men, held in 1956. In December 1982, the second world championships for women were held in Paris. In 1984, the third world championships for women were held in Vienna.

In April 1984, exactly one hundred and two years since judo was founded, the new Kodokan International Judo Centre was officially opened. This brand new eight storey building includes a grand dojo with 420 tatami and seating for 460 spectators. Smaller dojos include a school dojo with 240 tatami, an international division dojo with 192 tatami, a women's section dojo with 240 tatami and a smaller dojo with 66 tatami for special lessons. All change rooms are equipped with electronically operated lockers. All students must carry an electronic key card identification which is inserted into a machine to gain entry for training. There is dormitory style accommodation for visiting teams in both western and eastern style. There is a judo memorial hall, judo library, research centre (complete with video equipment), and a conference hall with seating for 100 people. Judo suits and equipment are sold in the entrance foyer, and there is a restaurant in the basement. The new Kodokan International Judo Centre is truly a judoka's dream.

History of Women's Judo in the World

Professor Jigoro Kano, the originator of judo, believed that one of the objectives of Japanese physical education should be the inclusion of females in the practice of judo, the main purpose being to teach women to defend themselves adequately. Therefore, more emphasis was placed upon teaching self-defence techniques.

In the long term, women would be more self confident and their physical and mental health would benefit enormously. At that time, just before the turn of the century, women were very modest indeed, especially women in Japan. Their kimono was very restrictive, their hair styles problematical for sport and, generally speaking, women of the middle and upper classes were extremely ladylike. From the very beginning Jigoro Kano realised that a different approach was required for females in judo, because of the physical and psychological differences of the sexes.

Miss Sueko Ashiya was recorded as the first girl to enter the judo classes in 1893 to study Kodokan judo personally from Jigoro Kano. Jigoro Kano later taught his own wife, Sumako, her personal friends and, later again, his eldest daughter, Noriko Watanuki (Kano), who was born in 1893 and who in her adult life became head of the Women's Section (*Joshi Bu*) of the Kodokan Judo Institute for many years.

Around 1905, Jigoro Kano founded a larger dojo in the Koubun Gakuin (School) in Tokyo, where several members from Nihon Women's University and Ochanomizu Girls' High School underwent much hard training. One of the most outstanding students of this time was Miss Kinko Yasuda, who was so enthusiastic that she undertook the task of making *judogi* of mikawa cotton for everyone in the women's group.

Judo became one of the main subjects of physical exercises in girls' schools and girls' Normal Schools in Japan by 1916. In November 1923, Mr Tomatsu Honda became the first instructor for women's judo at the Kodokan Judo Institute. In October 1926, female training was held for two weeks in the Kodokan dojo, where twelve disciples gathered from Hokkaido in the north of Japan, and Fukuoka and Nagasaki in the south. On 9 November 1926, the Kodokan originated a women's division (*Joshi Bu*), separate from the men's division, at the Kaiunzaka Hall under Tomatsu Honda, with Aiko Shiba as manager of the dojo.

In 1931, the Kodokan originated an oath book for all newly enrolled female students to sign. The first newcomer to sign this book was Masako Noritormi, then Miss Ayako Akutagawa and Miss Yasuko Morioka. The first name to appear on the *Yudanshakai* (black belt) roll book for women, in January 1933, was Katsuko Osaki. Others who followed afterwards were Noriko Watanuki (Kano), eldest daughter of Jigoro Kano, then Atsuko Takasaki, Hisako Miyagawa, Asako Okada, Kinko Yasuda and Utano Miyoshi, all of whom were personally instructed by Jigoro Kano before the official inception of the Women's Division (*Joshi Bu*) in 1926.

By 1945, women's judo had become quite firmly established and many women were gaining Yudansha (black belt) status. The growing popularity of judo in schools and women's universities was evident. Around this time, Miss Masako Noritormi, 5th dan, and Miss Keiko Fukuda, 4th dan, were instructing at the Kodokan Women's Division. Later Takahashi Sensei was appointed.

Jigoro Kano deliberated for many years about the physical and psychological differences of men and women in judo. Before his death, he laid the foundation of *joshi* judo (women's judo), based upon careful deliberation of the physical capacity and endurance levels of women. The katas he originated in 1887, such as *Ju-no-kata, Nage-no-kata, Katame-no-kata* and *Kime-no-kata,* have all been incorporated into the various dan grades of women's Yudansha requirements. In 1943, Jiro Nango (nephew of Jigoro Kano) originated *Goshin-ho* which is a women's self defence kata and is also part of the women's requirements in the kyu or novice grades. More specifically, Jigoro Kano suggested the techniques to be introduced at certain levels, gradually, so as not to frighten female practitioners before they were high enough in grade and experienced enough to cope with the more difficult techniques. Only when students were exceptionally confident in *ukemi-waza* or breakfalling were the more dangerous techniques introduced. Perfection in *zenpo-kaiten* or forward rolling was vitally important. Jigoro Kano considered the correct essence of *atemi-waza* or striking the vital points of the body very important in conjunction with developing self-confidence in self-defence movements and kata.

Randori was the vital link in overall perfection and execution of all throwing techniques. *Renraku-waza* (combination techniques) and *kaeshi-waza* (counter techniques) were considered to be an integral part of the overall perspective of *randori*. Because women are generally not as physically strong as men, he emphasised the importance of *tai-sabaki* (body turning and management), evasions and overall body prowess. At this stage, women did not participate in *shiai*, (competition judo).

About 1949, Miss Ruth Gardiner of Chicago, U.S.A., became the first foreign female student to study at the Kodokan Judo Institute, women's division. Miss Gardiner had been formerly taught judo by male instructors up to the *shodan* (first dan black belt). Her main objective in visiting Japan was to study for *nidan* (second degree or dan black belt).

Miss Collet from France was the second foreign female student to study at the *Joshi Bu* or women's division of the Kodokan Judo Institute and Miss Helen Carollo of Oakland, California, U.S.A., became the third. Since that time many women from all over the world have travelled to Japan especially to study *joshi* judo. Currently, there are no accommodation facilities at the Kodokan Judo Institute for visiting female foreign students, so the majority of women judoka usually live at the Tokyo Y.W.C.A., in the nearby Kanda district, whilst studying daily at the Kodokan. The Kodokan is being renovated and sections of the building are being rebuilt. This project commenced in 1982 and was completed in April, 1984. This brand new Kokokan International Judo Centre now has accommodation for female foreign students.

One of the first Kodokan *joshi sensei* (female instructors) to travel overseas to teach women's judo was Miss Keiko Fukuda, 7th dan, who travelled to Australia and the Philippines and later settled in the United States to live permanently. Miss Keiko Fukuda has travelled extensively to various states of America and also to Canada giving seminars on women's judo. The two highest graded Kodokan women in the world are Haruko Niboshi, 7th dan, (Chief Instructress of the Kodokan Judo Institute) and Miss Keiko Fukuda, 7th dan, of California, U.S.A. Miss Masako Noritormi was promoted to 7th dan prior to her death, after a prolonged illness, in 1981.

Most women in other countries of the world have been taught judo by male instructors, mainly because of the lack of qualified female instructors available in the world. Women were not permitted to play competition judo at international level until the first International Women's Judo Championships were held in Maddison Square Gardens, New York, in November 1980. The second International Women's Judo Championships were held in Paris in December 1982. Women are not yet included in the Olympic Games.

It is almost one hundred years since the inception of judo and almost ninety years since Jigoro Kano taught his first female student, Miss Sueko Ashiyama, in 1893. On an international level women's judo has not made great technical progress in that time. There is a serious lack of highly qualified female instructresses available in the world, and not many women are willing to dedicate their lives to teaching judo professionally.

The first women's judo federation ever to exist in the world was founded by Miss Patricia Harrington, 5th dan, and Mrs Betty Huxley, 4th dan, in 1968, for the purpose of propagating Kodokan *joshi* judo (women's judo) throughout Australia. Miss Patricia Harrington and Mrs Betty Huxley have received all of their dan or black belt grades from the Kodokan Judo Institute and since 1964 have made ten trips to Japan to study women's judo exclusively at the Kodokan Judo Institute. In 1970, Miss Harrington and Mrs Huxley founded the Australian Women's Yudanshakai (Black Belt Federation), which became the very first women's black belt federation to exist in the world. The members of the Australian Women's Judo Federation made a practice of studying all twelve aspects of judo, including competition judo (*shiai*), without allowing any single aspect to dominate, in order to have a balanced perspective of judo. They felt that the *shiai* aspect of judo has become so predominent that the technical side of judo has severely diminished. In March 1983, the Australian Women's Judo Federation and the Australian Women's Yudanshakai changed their names and joined the Australian authority for the International Judo Federation, the Judo Federation of Australia.

The future policies of women's judo have not yet been decided, but, essentially, women should consider practising all twelve aspects of judo, without neglecting any single part. Modern women in the 1980s are indeed considerably different from the modest women of Jigoro Kano Shihan's first group of ninety odd years ago. Each country has its cultural and political differences concerning women's behavioural patterns in sport, but, clearly, modern women, because of their freedom and participation in sport today, are stronger and psychologically more enthusiastic and daring than their predecessors. Only when women's judo is really correctly studied and taught by qualified instructors, will it be fully understood and real progress be made.

References
Kodokan Judo, Kodansha, Tokyo, Japan
Canon of Judo, K. Mifune

Born for the Mat, Keiko Fukuda
Illustrated Kodokan Judo, Kodansha Limited, Tokyo, Japan
Judo Kodokan, Nunoi Shobo C. Ltd, Osaka, Japan
Judo, British Judo Association
Standing Judo, Mikinosuke Kawaishi
The Fighting Spirit of Japan, E. J. Harrison
History of Judo in the World, Sanzo Maruyama

Structure of International Judo

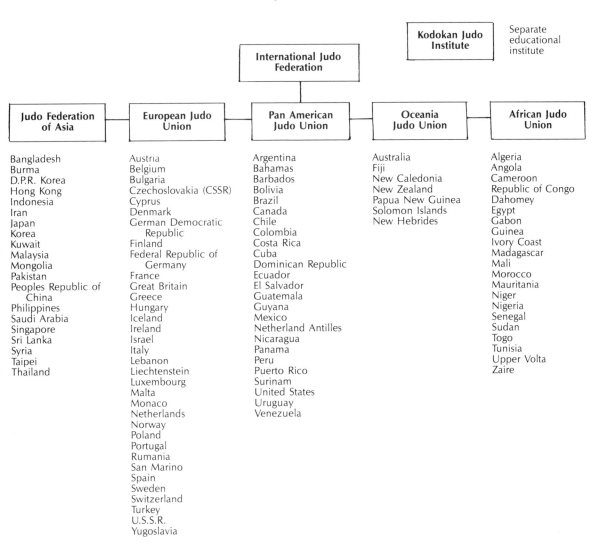

| Kodokan Judo Institute | Separate educational institute |

International Judo Federation

Judo Federation of Asia	European Judo Union	Pan American Judo Union	Oceania Judo Union	African Judo Union
Bangladesh	Austria	Argentina	Australia	Algeria
Burma	Belgium	Bahamas	Fiji	Angola
D.P.R. Korea	Bulgaria	Barbados	New Caledonia	Cameroon
Hong Kong	Czechoslovakia (CSSR)	Bolivia	New Zealand	Republic of Congo
Indonesia	Cyprus	Brazil	Papua New Guinea	Dahomey
Iran	Denmark	Canada	Solomon Islands	Egypt
Japan	German Democratic Republic	Chile	New Hebrides	Gabon
Korea		Colombia		Guinea
Kuwait	Finland	Costa Rica		Ivory Coast
Malaysia	Federal Republic of Germany	Cuba		Madagascar
Mongolia		Dominican Republic		Mali
Pakistan	France	Ecuador		Morocco
Peoples Republic of China	Great Britain	El Salvador		Mauritania
	Greece	Guatemala		Niger
Philippines	Hungary	Guyana		Nigeria
Saudi Arabia	Iceland	Mexico		Senegal
Singapore	Ireland	Netherland Antilles		Sudan
Sri Lanka	Israel	Nicaragua		Togo
Syria	Italy	Panama		Tunisia
Taipei	Lebanon	Peru		Upper Volta
Thailand	Liechtenstein	Puerto Rico		Zaire
	Luxembourg	Surinam		
	Malta	United States		
	Monaco	Uruguay		
	Netherlands	Venezuela		
	Norway			
	Poland			
	Portugal			
	Rumania			
	San Marino			
	Spain			
	Sweden			
	Switzerland			
	Turkey			
	U.S.S.R.			
	Yugoslavia			

Introduction to Judo

The first impression is of vital importance to the student beginning judo.

Enrolment

The first procedure is usually the process of enrolment. When a student fills out an enrolment form to commence judo training, the conditions and by-laws should be clearly explained. Judo and other martial arts are first and foremost discipline sports.

By-laws of Discipline

Punctuality.

Total observance of hygiene.

Courtesy and respect at all times in the dojo to one's instructor and to all other judoka.

Regular attendance at all instruction and training sessions.

Training and membership fees must be promptly paid.

Once students have accepted these conditions and have duly signed the enrolment form and membership application, they have virtually pledged themselves to uphold these by-laws while they remain practitioners of the art of judo. Violation of the rules will surely result in disciplinary measures from the instructor, for there is no place in judo for disrespectful students. Many young people today very much resent discipline and having to conform to rules and regulations. Such persons have no right to expect to become judokas, let alone attain higher degrees in judo. Judo degrees, especially *yudansha* or black belt, should only be awarded to the most serious practitioners, who have worked many long hours and years, readily accepting the advice of their instructors with gratitude. To be successful in judo, the student must respect authority, whether it be monarchical, hierarchical, governmental, or institutional, and believe in the somewhat old-fashioned virtues—honour, valour, integrity, honesty, decency and the like.

Principles and Aims

The first principle one learns in Kodokan judo is that of *ju* or gentleness. In fact, it is this syllable *ju*, combined with the syllable *do*, meaning 'way', which comprises the meaning of the name *judo* or 'gentle way'.

To understand this first principle correctly, one must learn the first motto, 'Best use of energy', or 'Maximum efficiency, minimum effort'. These mottos constantly expounded by the originator of judo, Jigoro Kano, Shihan, are best explained as follows:

If one's partner suddenly pulls with a very strong force, one must learn to go with the strong pull, instead of resisting it and, in doing so, add one's own strength to the initial force by pushing, so doubling the momentum of the said force. If on the other hand, one becomes stubborn and allows one's mind to remain unpliable, then the natural response when pushed, would be to resist and push back, resulting in the immediate neutralisation of technique, or being locked in a position of stalemate. To resist or block the initiation of the technique is indeed a bad habit in judo and is against the first basic principle of *ju*. To learn to yield to an oncoming force gives rise to creation of technique and blends the combined forces into a beautiful harmony, once set in motion. To keep this harmony of technique in motion is a natural extension and maintenance of the basic principle of *ju*, which ultimately leads to the perfection of all underlying principles of judo and in addition to the achievement of a balance of harmony within the mind and body of the judo student, which is the highest goal of achievement spoken of by the originator of judo, Jigoro Kano, Shihan.

If one dedicates oneself entirely to the perfection of the basic principles in judo, obtaining rank is only of secondary importance. One must aspire then, if one becomes an instructor, to pass on this knowledge in its purest form, to as many sincere followers as possible. It is essential to understand the second most important maxim, 'Mutual welfare and benefit', so that judo can be clearly understood and practised by young and old alike, benefiting mind and body all the days of one's life. To develop pliability of mind and body is a goal spoken of by the originator of judo. Cultivating the correct attitude and approach to judo, based on these basic principles, will take many, many years of daily dedication and training and indeed the pitfalls are many, but in the long term, those who persevere will ultimately be rewarded, not only in rank, but also in a deeper understanding of the art of judo which serves as a philosophy and a way of life and results in a consolidation of philosophical principle which serves one in his senior years of judo, when the prowess of youth has diminished.

If one begins to study judo and is made constantly aware of the basic philosophy based on the famous maxims of Jigoro Kano, Shihan, then it naturally follows that one will develop the correct attitude to training for the chapters to follow.

The Dojo or Training Hall

This room should be used exclusively for judo when the classes are in session. The dojo should be imbued with a solemn atmosphere. It should be properly ventilated, spotlessly clean and adequately lighted. There should be a *joseki*, or official platform, upon which hangs a portrait of the originator of judo, Jigoro Kano, Shihan.

No noise or frivolity should be permitted in the dojo, and the students should be disciplined to bow solemnly, with respect, to the *joseki* upon entering the dojo and practise quietly until the instructor summons the class to assemble and begin training.

All classes should be bowed in correctly at the beginning of a session and bowed out correctly at the conclusion of a session, and the correct dojo decorum should be maintained throughout the training or instruction session. The students must be on their best behaviour at all times in the dojo and set a high standard of discipline. The higher-graded students are expected to set an example whilst in the dojo for the lower-graded students to follow. The instructor in charge of the dojo must command the respect and discipline of all students at all times.

Tatami   Correct judo mat

The tatami are traditional straw mats, approximately six feet long, three feet wide and two inches in thickness. Tatami are covered with a non-slip vinyl for hygienic purposes. In a traditional japanese dojo, the tatami are placed upon correctly constructed sprung floors, whereas most overseas judo clubs have the tatami laid down on an ordinary wooden floor and held together with mat brackets made of one inch tubular steel, held in place with horizontal and vertical straps, or alternatively wooden brackets. This equipment is removed and stacked away in storage cupboards after each judo training session is finished, because the gymnasium is used for other sporting activities.

To maintain tatami, mop them over with a damp disinfected mop. There are other types of mats being used for judo all over the world and quite often judo is taught on gymnastic mats, wrestling maps, canvas covered mats and substitute tatami filled with foam solid and covered with vinyl.

Judogi

One should never practice judo unless one is wearing the correct garment, the judogi. Home made substitutes or karategi are not correct and will tear easily and can cause injuries. The judogi for women is the same as that worn by men. In Japan the only difference is that the trousers on some women's judogi are gathered in at the bottom of the trouser legs, drawing them in around the ankles.

Basically the judogi consists of a jacket, pants or trousers and a belt. All women are expected to wear a white cotton tee shirt or singlet underneath their judogi. The judogi is traditionally white or off white in colour including the beginner's belt. The colour of the belt changes as one progresses in grade and also according to one's age, that is to say, junior grades, adolescent and adult grades. Women generally wear a thin white stripe throughout the entire length of their belt, which indicates female grade (please refer to the ranking system).

When purchasing a judogi, one must realise that the shrinkage rate must be taken into consideration. After the new garment has been washed in a normal washing machine using hot water and normal powdered or liquid soap, the eventual size of the judogi should be such that the trousers come down to the bottom of the ankles, and the jacket sleeves should come down to the bottom of the wrists. The jacket should come down over the hips and should feel loose and comfortable. When in constant use, the judogi should be washed regularly, pressed and mended whenever necessary.

Usually, the club emblem is worn on the right lapel of the judogi, because the left lapel is constantly being grasped in the normal method of holding the jacket.

How to Wear the Judogi
When putting on the trousers, the knee pads sewn into the pants are worn at the front. After stepping into the pants, pull both draw strings at the back until the pants are drawn in sufficiently to be worn comfortably, then proceed to tie off the cords, by looping them through the loops provided and tie into a bow securely.

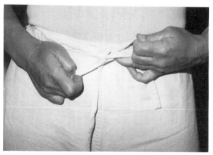

The jacket is worn by closing the left lapel over the right.

The Correct Method of Tying the Belt or *Obi*

Find the centre of the belt by holding it up, place the belt onto your waist. Proceed to draw both ends outwards in preparation to wrap them around.

As you pass both ends of the belt around, pass one layer under the other and proceed to return the ends to the front again.

Tighten the belt to the required tightness, then pass the end in your right hand under both layers or thicknesses of the belt.

Pass the end in your right hand under and through the end in your left.

Pull through and adjust the knot until both ends of the belt are exactly the same length.

Additional Equipment Required

Dojo slippers or sandles must be worn at all times in the corridors leading into the dojo or training hall and must be slipped off at the edge of the mat area, or tatami and placed neatly alongside all other slippers. The student's name should be marked clearly on his sandles. This is traditional in all correctly conducted dojos, to ensure that the tatami area is kept spotlessly clean. The instructor reserves the right to inspect the cleanliness of the student's feet and the regulation cut of the toe nails at any time prior to each class commencing.

Protective Equipment

For the judo beginner, it is important to wear shin guards to protect the lower ankles and shins from severe bruising, because in the early stages of learning judo, skill in sweeping with the feet is not yet correctly developed.

Men and boys should wear a groin guard to all judo classes.

Dojo Towel

All judo students are permitted to carry a dojo towel to wipe away the perspiration during training. The dojo towel may be worn around one's neck during training breaks in order to keep in the body heat, and should be left folded neatly on the side of the dojo when training. Wiping one's face on the sleeve of one's judogi, or flicking off one's perspiration onto the tatami is considered very bad dojo behaviour.

Judogi Training Bag or Gi Bag

The judogi and all necessary equipment mentioned above should be carried to judo classes in a training bag, or gi bag. It is always a good idea to include a bandage and some band-aids in case of minor injuries.

Always leave your dojo sandles and belt in the bottom of your gi bag permanently and you will never arrive at your judo classes without these essential items. Your name should be marked inside your judogi, both the jacket and pants, and on all personal equipment. The judogi must not be worn in public, except when one participates in a public exhibition. Therefore, carry your judogi, sandles, towel, protective equipment and whatever else you require in your training or gi bag.

Judo Grading or Ranking System

Yonen Grade (age 12 years and under)

Yonen Rank	Japanese Colour
6th or *Rok-kyu*	White
5th or *Go-kyu*	White
4th or *Yon-kyu*	White
3rd or *San-kyu*	Green
2nd or *Ni-kyu*	Green
1st or *Ik-kyu*	Green

Conversion to Shonen Rank at 13 years of age

Shonen Rank	Japanese Colour
. . . . .	. . . . .
. . . . .	. . . . .
Rok-kyu	White
Go-kyu	White
Yon-kyu	White
San-kyu	Purple

Shonen Grade (age 16 years and under)

Shonen Rank	Japanese Colour
6th or *Rok-kyu*	White
5th or *Go-kyu*	White
4th or *Yon-kyu*	White
3rd or *San-kyu*	Purple
2nd or *Ni-kyu*	Purple
1st or *Ik-kyu*	Purple

Conversion to Seinen Rank at 17 years of age

Seinen Rank	Japanese Colour
. . . . .	. . . . .
. . . . .	. . . . .
Rok-kyu	White
Go-kyu	White
Yon-kyu	White
San-kyu	Brown

Kyu or Student Grade (*Mudansha*)

Rank	Japanese Colour	Japanese Colour	European Colour
	Junior (Under 15 years)	Senior	Seniors and Juniors
6th or *Rok-kyu*	Turquoise	White	White
5th or *Go-kyu*	White	White	Yellow
4th or *Yon-kyu*	White	White	Orange
3rd or *San-kyu*	Purple	Brown	Green
2nd or *Ni-kyu*	Purple	Brown	Blue
1st or *Ik-kyu*	Purple	Brown	Brown

Dan or Master Grade (*Yudansha*) — Adult Grade (17 years and over)

Rank	Japanese Colour	European Colour	Female Colour
1st dan—*Shodan*	Black	Black	Black with white line lengthwise
2nd dan—*Nidan*	Black	Black	Black with white line lengthwise
3rd dan—*Sandan*	Black	Black	Black with white line lengthwise
4th dan—*Yondan*	Black	Black	Black with white line lengthwise
5th dan—*Godan*	Black	Black	Black with white line lengthwise
6th dan—*Rokudan*	Red and White	Red and White	
7th dan—*Shichidan*	Red and White	Red and White	
8th dan—*Hachidan*	Red and White	Red and White	
9th dan—*Kudan*	Red	Red	
10th dan—*Judan*	Red	Red	

The Correct Method of Bowing

Because judo originated in Japan, the art is steeped in the tradition of bowing or correct salutation. Judo classes begin and end with the correct salutation. From the very first lesson, the beginner is taught how to bow correctly.

The correct attitude to bowing displays excellence of good manners and the bow should be executed in a solemn and graceful way. Whether bowing to the *joseki* or official platform in the dojo, or to the dojo *sensei*, or to one's training partner, the posture of bowing should depict mutual respect.

Standing bow *Ritsurei*

To execute *ritsurei* correctly, bring your heels together, toes apart and hands open and pressed against the upper thighs.

Bend over slowly from the waist, then return to an upright posture once again.

Ritsurei is an informal bow which is used constantly during practice and should be practised until the bow can be executed smoothly and not in a jerky or clumsy manner.

The Kneeling Bow *Zarei*

Kneel down on the left knee setting the toes of the left foot. The toes of the right foot should be in line with the left knee.

Kneel down on the right knee and both feet have the toes in a set position.

Slide your hands off the upper thighs as you bend forward slowly and place them onto the tatami approximately six centimeters apart. Bow your head as low as possible, then return to an upright posture again.

When coming up to standing, proceed to set the toes of both feet, then bring the right knee up with the toes of the right foot in line with the left knee. Then bring the left knee up and come back up to standing again.

Unset your toes and cross the right big toe over the left and sit back onto your heels with your feet flat underneath, sitting correctly in the *seiza* posture.

Basic Postures of Judo

Basic Natural Posture
Shizen-hontai The basic posture is maintained by standing in a relaxed attitude, the feet should be approximately twelve inches apart and the arms held loosely at the sides.

Right Natural Posture
Migi-shizentai Stand with the right foot advanced about twelve inches.

Left Natural Posture
Hidari-shizentai Stand with the left foot advanced about twelve inches.

Basic Defensive Posture
Jigo-hontai Stand with both feet level and approximately thirty inches apart, the knees should be bent and the hips slightly lowered.

Right Defensive Posture
Migi-jigotai Advance the right foot forward. The feet should be approximately thirty inches apart, the knees bent and the hips lowered.

Left Defensive Posture
Hidari-jigotai Advance the left foot forward by approximately two feet. The feet should be about thirty inches apart.

The Correct Method of Grasping the Opponent's Jacket *Kumi-kata*

The basic grip on the judogi is the same for both partners. Engage in *Shizen-hontai*, the basic natural posture and both opponents should proceed to grasp each other's left lapel with the right hand so that the thumb grips inside the left lapel and the four fingers close the grip. Then both proceed to grasp each other's right sleeve with the left hand closing the hand naturally. It is essential that the grip is not too tight. It should be noted that the position of the holds on the jacket may be reversed to any of the permitted parts of the judogi according to the required effect of the action when the student has mastered the use of this basic hold or grip on all throws.

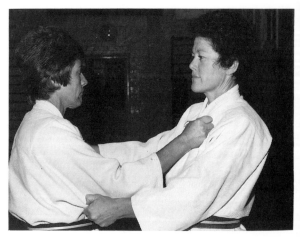

opponent, *tsugi-ashi*, succeeding or following foot, must be used. In this technique one foot is used as the leading foot, whilst the rear foot is drawn up. This is repeated for several movements forwards and then backwards. When practising *tsugi-ashi* the step should not be executed too wide, nor should the feet be brought together.

Tai-sabaki, the management of the body, is concerned with the turning movement or action of the body. It is vitally important to develop speed in turning in movements of the body for *randori* or contest in order to maintain a balanced posture.

Use of the Feet in Movement *Shintai* and *Tai-sabaki*

The word *shintai* is best translated as 'movement'. This means the manner of advancing or retreating, or moving to the right or to the left of the original position.

In general, whenever the body is moved forwards or backwards, to either side, or turned in any direction, the weight of the body should be over the leading foot. When close to the

Happo-kuzushi Breaking of Balance

Maushiro
or
Backwards

Migiatosumi
or
Right back corner

Hidariatosumi
or
Left back corner

Migiyoko
or
Right side

Hidariyoko
or
Left side

Migimaesumi
or
Right front corner

Hidarimaesumi
or
Left front corner

Manmae
or
Front

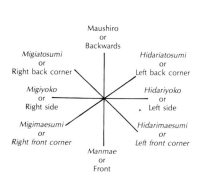

Standing with heels together, toes apart, exchange a standing bow. Both opponents step forward with the left foot, then the right.

Both opponents grasp each other's left lapel with the right hand, and each other's sleeve with the left hand.

Manmae Kuzushi Direct front corner. Tori breaks Uke's balance directly forward.

Maushiro Kuzushi Direct back corner. Tori breaks Uke's balance directly backwards.

Migiyoko Kuzushi Tori breaks Uke's balance directly to Uke's right side.

Hidariyoko Kuzushi Tori breaks Uke's balance directly to Uke's left side.

Migimaesumi Right front corner. Tori breaks Uke's balance to Uke's right front corner.

Hidarimaesumi Left front corner. Tori breaks Uke's balance to Uke's left front corner.

Migiatosumi Right back corner. Tori breaks Uke's balance to Uke's right back corner.

Hidariatosumi Left back corner. Tori breaks Uke's balance to Uke's left back corner.

Warming Up for Judo

Calisthenics have almost been phased out of the warming up routines in judo, and replaced with stretching exercises. However, most stretching exercises are performed in similar positions to calisthenics. Everybody should warm up correctly before training. It is essential to loosen all joints in addition to stretching all muscles of the body prior to hard training. Warming up routines increase the blood supply to the muscles and raise their temperature. It is a good idea to have a set routine, such as starting with the neck muscles, then the shoulders, the spine, hips, and so forth until you reach the ankles. If you systematically loosen all joints from head to toe and stretch all muscles attached to these joints, your body will respond more readily to the demands about to be made upon it.

Muscle tightness is usually caused by hard exercise. When you stretch, do it slowly and gently, and hold each position for ten to thirty seconds. Avoid quick, jerky movements. Tight muscles are more susceptible to injury. Stretching improves flexibility and prevents injury.

Many sports psychologists use the warm up routine to reassure their athletes before top performances. If you are suffering from tight muscles from a previous training session, it is strongly advisable to get into the dojo early and stretch your body slowly so that you gradually warm up your sore muscles and loosen up your tight joints and sore spots, and literally psyche yourself into preparation for another hard work-out. The best cure for sore muscles is to rewarm and gently stretch your body systematically. If your physical condition is poor, you will suffer until you become physically fit. Nobody can take hard training sessions unless gradually physically and psychologically prepared for them.

Rotate your head around in circular movements to each side gently.

Stretch your head first in a backwards position for five to ten seconds and repeat several times.

Tuck your chin onto your chest and stretch your neck muscles forward for five to ten seconds and repeat several times.

Swing both arms forward and rotate several times over forward and back to loosen the shoulder joints.

Stretch your shoulder back as far as possible for ten seconds, then repeat on the opposite side.

Raise your elbow over and stretch for five to ten seconds, then repeat on the opposite side.

Stretching both legs as far open as possible.

Stretch backwards for five seconds, then forward for five to ten seconds, then to the right and left side respectively. Repeat this sequence several times.

Stretching from left to right.

Raise both arms overhead and stretch left and right sides for ten seconds each side.

Body twisting or turning to loosen the spinal area. Turn to both sides, holding for up to ten seconds each side.

Rotate your pelvis in large circular movements left and right sides.

Lunge from side to side, holding each position for up to ten seconds. Lunge as low as possible and press firmly against the hip joint.

Ten second stretches forward and left and right sides respectively. Repeat several times.

Perform push up movements slowly and strongly. Eliminate any jerky movements.

Three second scoop ups. Perform a scoop up movement over the duration of three seconds. Repeat at least twenty times.

Raise your legs up slowly over the period of five seconds. Repeat at least ten times.

Lower your legs slowly over the period of five seconds and turn the soles of your feet inwards to increase dexterity.

Finish off the warming up sequence by rotating each ankle firmly and slowly, then move the toes of each foot forward and backwards several times.

References

The Sportsmedicine Book, Gabe Mirkin, M.D., Marshall Hoffman, Lansdowne

The Sports Medicine Guide, Dr Mark E. Wolpa, Leisure Press, New York

Stretching, Bob Anderson, Shelter Publications, Inc., Bolinas, California, U.S.A.

Breakfalling

Ukemi   Basic Breakfalling

Lying flat on your back and keeping your head up, raise both legs upwards then strike the tatami at a forty-five degree angle to the body with the palms of both hands.

Practice to alternate sides, breakfalling with the feet and hands simultaneously. If breakfalling with the right hand, then the sole of the left foot will also hit the tatami, then alternate to the opposite side so that the left hand makes a breakfall and the sole of the right foot hits the tatami. Note that the head must be kept up and the hands make a breakfall at approximately forty-five degrees to the body.

1

2

Breakfalling backwards from a sitting position. Raise both hands, then proceed to fall backwards, keeping your chin onto your chest and head up. Counterbalance your legs upwards as you simultaneosly hit the tatami at a forty-five degree angle to the body with both hands. Breakfalling backwards can also be practised left and right side respectively.

1

Breakfalling backwards from a squatting position. Raise both hands forward, ensure that you tuck your chin onto your chest and keep your head up, and fall backwards. Strike the tatami at forty-five degree angles to your body with the palms of both hands and counterbalance your legs upright.

2

Squatting breakfall right side
Squatting on the left leg, advance the right foot and right hand forward. Slide the right foot and right hand across and lower the right hip onto the tatami.

Swing both legs upwards and breakfall with the right hand, palm downwards at a forty-five degree angle to your body.

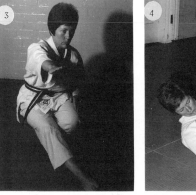

From a standing position advance the right foot and extend the right hand.

Slide the right foot across in front of your body and bend the left leg.

Squat down on the left leg and lower the right hip onto the tatami. Continue the swing of both legs upwards into a counterbalance position and strike the tatami with the palm of the right hand simultaneously at a forty-five degree angle to your body.

Zenpo-kaiten   Rolling Forward

Commence by placing the right foot forward. Place the right hand in line with the right foot with the wrist turned backwards. Place the left hand facing forward.

Tuck your head in and lean forward establishing momentum and trying to keep your legs straight in flight.

Breakfall with the palm of the left hand and the sole of the right foot on impact.

Terminate in a lying down posture.

Place the right foot forward and the right hand in line turned backwards. Place the left hand in line facing forward.

Tuck your head in and lean forward establishing momentum. Try to keep your legs straight in flight.

Breakfall with the palm of the left hand and the sole of the right foot simultaneously and

terminate in a standing posture.

Backwards Breakfall

Walk backwards several paces, then take a squatting backwards position with arms raised. Fall backwards and breakfall with both hands, palms down, and creating backwards momentum pass your right leg over your right shoulder, turning your head inwards. Terminate on your right knee with your left leg extended and toes set. Alternativly, terminate in a standing up position.

Falling Forward

For beginners just learning this breakfall, it is better to start in a kneeling position.

Advanced judo students practise the fall from a standing position.

Fall forward, breakfalling with the palms of both hands and support yourself with the forearms and toes extended.

The Kodokan *Gokyo-no-waza*

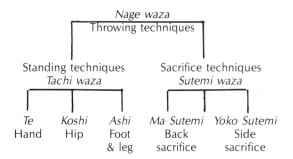

The Kodokan *Gokyo-no-waza* contains five sets of throwing techniques. Each set contains eight throws. These courses of instruction, together, contain forty techniques.

The key to teaching the *Gokyo-no-waza* varies according to the type of group one is teaching, for example, children's judo, *yonen* (under 13 years of age) or *shonen* (under 16 years of age) or adults.

It is important, especially when teaching young children, to teach the most simple throws first, i.e. those applied to the lowest point of the ankle. When the beginner is reasonably confident in falling and throwing correctly in such techniques as *Sasae-tsurikomi-ashi* and *De-ashi-harai*, then the instructor would introduce such techniques as *O-soto-gari*, which is applied to the back of the calf muscle and *Hiza-guruma*, which is applied to the knee and so on. These relatively simple throws are the easiest techniques for beginners to learn first and more importantly to learn to breakfall from correctly and safely.

As the beginner's confidence begins to improve and his or her standard of breakfalling increases, the more difficult techniques can be introduced.

Instruction 1

1. *De-ashi-harai* (Advanced Foot Sweep)
2. *Hiza-guruma* (Knee Wheel)
3. *Sasae-tsurikomi-ashi* (Propping Drawing Ankle Throw)
4. *Uki-goshi* (Floating Hip or Loin)
5. *O-soto-gari* (Major Outer Reaping)
6. *O-goshi* (Major Loin)
7. *O-uchi-gari* (Major Inner Reaping)
8. *Seoi-nage* (Shoulder Throw)

Instruction 2

9. *Ko-soto-gari* (Minor Outer Reaping Ankle Throw)
10. *Ko-uchi-gari* (Minor Inner Reaping Ankle Throw)
11. *Koshi-guruma* (Loin Wheel)
12. *Tsurikomi-goshi* (Lift-pull Loin)
13. *Okuri-ashi-harai* (Sweeping Ankle Throw)
14. *Tai-otoshi* (Body Drop)
15. *Harai-goshi* (Sweeping Loin)
16. *Uchi-mata* (Inner Thigh)

Instruction 3

17. *Ko-soto-gake* (Minor Outer Hooking Angle Throw)
18. *Tsuri-goshi* (Lifting Hip Throw)
19. *Yoko-otoshi* (Side Drop)
20. *Ashi-guruma* (Leg Wheel)
21. *Hane-goshi* (Spring-hip Throw)
22. *Harai-tsurikomi-ashi* (Sweeping Drawing Ankle Throw)

| 23. | *Tomoe-nage* | (Throwing in High Circle or Stomach Throw) |
| 24. | *Kata-guruma* | (Shoulder Wheel) |

Instruction 4

25.	*Sumigaeshi*	(Corner Throw)
26.	*Tani-otoshi*	(Valley Drop)
27.	*Hane-makikomi*	(Outer Winding Spring Hip)
28.	*Sukui-nage*	(Scooping Throw)
29.	*Utsuri-goshi*	(Changing Hip)
30.	*O-guruma*	(Major Wheel)
31.	*Soto-makikomi*	(Outer Winding Throw)
32.	*Uki-otoshi*	(Floating Drop)

Instruction 5

33.	*O-soto-guruma*	(Major Outer Wheel)
34.	*Uki-waza*	(Floating Throw)
35.	*Yoko-wakare*	(Side-separation)
36.	*Yoko-guruma*	(Side Wheel)
37.	*Ushiro-goshi*	(Rear Loin)
38.	*Ura-nage*	(Rear Throw)
39.	*Sumi-otoshi*	(Corner Drop)
40.	*Yoko-gake*	(Side Body Drop)

Composition of a Throwing Technique

1. **Kuzushi** To break the opponent's balance, or body posture, in preparation for a throw.
2. **Tsukuri** To position one's body relevant to the intended technique.
3. **Kake** The actual moment of attack, or of throwing the opponent.

Kuzushi It is quite essential, when attempting a throwing technique, to disturb your opponent's posture correctly before making the actual attack. There are eight methods of *kuzushi* based on the basic natural posture. One must practise the correct method of breaking the opponent's balance by pushing or pulling in straight or curved lines, as well as in every direction, making the opponent lose balance effectively. These eight basic methods of *kuzushi* are indispensable factors of the correct techniques of judo.

Tsukuri Having broken your opponent's balance it is vital to be able to hold yourself ready at the same time to attack and position your body relevant to the intended technique, to actually apply your contemplated technique. One needs to cultivate a very supple and pliable body and dexterity of the feet. Studying the biomechanics, or kinesiology of the human body will provide one with an insight into the positions into which one must manipulate one's body in order to successfully apply *tsukuri*. In judo, one is actually lifting live body weight, which, if not correctly timed and manipulated, can result in bad injuries, to both the person throwing, and to the person falling. It is essential to develop excellent *tai-sabaki* or body turning in movements, with skill and speed.

Kake *Kake* is the actual attack, or moment of throwing, which needs a quick explosive action in order to direct and manipulate, with skill, the opponent's body into the desired position of falling with absolute safety. Throwing an opponent with skill requires a complete understanding of the principle behind a throwing technique.

True technical judo requires many years of constant study to understand all of the ramifications, let alone to perfect them and furthermore to remain constantly proficient in all forty throws of the *Gokyo-no-waza*.

Uke and Tori

Uke is the partner who is receiving the technique and who will make the breakfall. *Tori* is the partner who is executing the technique or throwing.

References
Kodokan Illustrated Judo, Kodansha
Kinesiology, Cooper & Glassow, Mosby

Instruction 1

De-ashi-harai (Advanced Foot Sweep)

Tori Move your partner's balance backwards.

Tori Sweep Uke's right ankle with the sole of your left foot and continue pulling Uke off balance.

Tori As Uke turns into a breakfall support Uke with a strong grip on the judogi.

Tori As Uke is landing, ensure a strong pull up on the judogi. Uke is responsible for the correct amount of pull down, so as not to hit the head when landing.

De-ashi-harai, the advanced foot sweep, can be applied as Uke is moved backwards, or as Uke is drawn forward by one step. However, for beginners, it is easier to learn the above method of applying the technique as Uke is moved backwards, then as one advances in grade, learn to apply the technique as Uke is drawn forward.

Hiza-guruma (Knee Wheel)

Tori Break Uke's balance to Uke's right front corner. Turn your right foot inwards and place the sole of your left foot on Uke's right knee.

Tori Throw Uke directly to Uke's right front corner, maintaining control of the throw with strong support on Uke's jacket.

Sasae-tsurikomi-ashi (Propping Drawing Ankle Throw)

Tori Break Uke's balance to Uke's right front corner. Turn your right foot inwards, and place the sole of your left foot against Uke's right ankle. Draw outwards with both arms.

Tori Throw Uke directly to Uke's right front corner, maintaining strong control of the throw and supporting Uke with a strong grip on the judogi.

Uki-goshi (Floating Hip or Loin)

Tori Break Uke's balance forward to Uke's right front corner and make an entry with the right foot towards Uke's right foot.

Tori Execute a body turning in movement as you place your right arm around Uke's waist. Continue the turning movement, creating more speed, and spin Uke forward.

O-soto-gari (Major Outer Reaping)

Tori Break Uke's balance backwards to the right back corner as you simultaneously advance your left foot forward.

Tori Continue to draw Uke's balance outwards as you reap your right leg to the back of Uke's right leg, throwing Uke backwards.

O-goshi (Major Loin)

Tori Break Uke's balance forward to the right front corner, as you simultaneously advance your right foot towards Uke's right foot.

Tori Make a body turning in entry and place your right arm tightly around Uke's waist. Make sure that your feet are inside Uke's feet.

Tori Throw your partner forward with a fast explosive action.

O-uchi-gari (Major Inner Reaping)

Tori Break Uke's balance backwards as you simultaneously reap your right foot through and around Uke's lower leg.

Tori Push Uke backwards.
Uke Execute a backward breakfall, slapping the tatami with both hands and counter-balance the legs.

Seoi-nage (Shoulder Throw) (Ippon Seoi-nage)

Tori Break Uke's balance forward as you simultaneously advance your right foot towards Uke's right foot.

Tori Make a body turning in movement as you simultaneously pass your right arm under Uke's right arm gripping Uke's judogi.

Tori Throw with a fast explosive action forward.

Eri-seoi-nage (Morote Seoi-nage)

Tori Break Uke's balance forward, as you simultaneously enter your right foot towards Uke's right foot.

Tori Make a body turning in movement as you simultaneously bend your right arm and place it under Uke's right armpit.

Tori Throw Uke forward with speed and force.

Instruction 2

Ko-soto-gari (Minor Outer Reaping Ankle Throw)

Tori Break your opponent's balance to her right back corner as you simultaneously advance your left foot forward and bring up your right foot. Reap the back of the opponent's right heel with your left foot.

Uke is thrown backwards.

Ko-uchi-gari (Minor Inner Reaping Ankle Throw)

Tori Break the opponent's balance to her right back corner as you simultaneously reap the opponent's right foot from the inside.

Uke will fall to the right back corner, breakfalling with both hands.

45

Koshi-guruma (Loin Wheel)

Tori Break your opponent's balance to his right front corner as you simultaneously advance your right foot towards the opponent's right foot.

Tori Make a body turning in entry placing your right arm around the opponent's neck and placing your hips tightly in position. Make sure your right hip projects out past Uke's hip.

Tori Throw Uke directly forward, over your hips, with speed and force.

Tsurikomi-goshi (Lift-pull Loin)

Tori Break the opponent's balance to her right front corner. Advance your right foot towards the opponent's right foot.

Tori Turn your body into position as you simultaneosly place your right forearm underneath Uke's left armpit.

Tori Sink your hips low and turn your body as you explosively throw Uke with force and speed directly forward.

Okuri-ashi-harai (Sweeping Ankle Throw)

Tori Advance your right foot forward, causing Uke to retreat backwards on the left foot.

Tori Take a wide left step as you advance your right foot inwards to support your body weight.

Tori Break Uke's balance to the right side and simultaneously sweep Uke's feet together as you lift Uke upwards.

Tori Throw Uke with speed and force.

Tai-otoshi (Body Drop)

Tori Break the opponent's balance to her right front corner. Advance your right foot towards Uke's right foot.

Tori Position your body so that your right foot blocks Uke's right ankle.

Tori Throw Uke directly forward with speed and force.

47

Harai-goshi (Sweeping Loin)

Tori Break the opponent's balance to her right front corner and simultaneously advance your right foot towards Uke's right foot.

Tori Continue to swing your body into position so that the left foot is positioned in the centre of gravity. Sweep the back of your right thigh against the front of Uke's right thigh.

Tori Throw Uke directly forward.

Uchi-mata (Inner Thigh)

Tori Break the opponent's balance forward to her right front corner. Advance your right foot towards Uke's right foot.

Tori Make a body turning in movement so that the left foot is positioned in the centre of gravity. Sweep your right thigh upwards on the inside of Uke's right thigh.

Tori Throw Uke directly forward.

Instruction 3

Ko-soto-gake (Minor Outer Hooking Ankle Throw)

Tori Break the opponent's balance to her right back corner. Advance your left foot forward.

Tori Draw up your right foot and simultaneously hook the sole of your left foot behind Uke's right heal reaping it upwards.

Uke will be thrown backwards towards the right back corner.

Ko-soto-gake is a modification of *Ko-soto-gari*. In former days it was regarded as a variety of *Ko-soto-gari*, but now it is classified as an independent technique.

Tsuri-goshi (Lifting Hip Throw)

Tori Break the opponent's balance to his right front corner. Advance your right foot towards Uke's right foot.

Tori Make a body turning in movement and simultaneously place your right arm around Uke's waist and grasp Uke's belt.

Uke will be thrown directly forward.

Yoko-otoshi (Side drop)

Tori Break your opponent's balance to her right side. Drop onto your left side as you simultaneously advance your left leg across Uke's right leg.

Tori Throw Uke with speed and force to Uke's right side.

Ashi-guruma (Leg Wheel)

Tori Break your opponent's balance to her right front corner. Move your left foot towards Uke's left foot.

Tori Swing your body in and simultaneously place the outside edge of your right foot against Uke's right knee.

Tori Throw Uke in a large circle over your leg.

Hane-goshi (Spring Hip Throw)

Tori Break your opponent's balance forward to her right front corner. Advance your right foot towards Uke's right foot.

Tori Make a body turning in movement and raise your right leg inside of Uke's right leg.

Tori Throw Uke with an explosive action directly forward.

Harai-tsurikomi-ashi (Sweeping Drawing Ankle Throw)

Tori Advance your right foot forward by one step causing Uke to retreat the left foot.

Tori Break your opponent's balance forward to her right front corner as you simultaneously sweep Uke's right foot with the sole of your left foot.

Tori Throw Uke with force and speed.

51

Tomoe-nage (Throwing in High Circle or Stomach Throw)

1. Engage in right natural posture.

2. *Tori* Advance your left foot to centre and break your opponent's balance forward.

3. *Tori* Throw yourself onto your back and simultaneously place your right foot onto Uke's right side lower abdomen.

4. Taking off on the right foot, Uke makes a right side forward rolling breakfall, terminating standing up.

Kata-guruma (Shoulder Wheel)

Engage in right natural posture.
Tori Draw Uke forward one pace on the right foot as you step back one pace with the left foot.

Tori Simultaneously change your left hand grip on Uke's judogi to an inside sleeve grip.

Tori Draw your left foot open as you break your opponent's balance forward to her right front corner.

Tori Advance your right foot in and bend underneath Uke's body, wrapping your right arm around Uke's right leg.

Tori As you straighten up close the left foot to the right.

Tori Throw Uke forward to your left front corner.

Instruction 4

Sumigaeshi (Corner Throw)

Tori and Uke engage in right defensive posture.

Tori Draw Uke forward one step. Uke advances the left foot whilst Tori retreats the right foot.

Tori Slide your left foot to centre and raise your right heel, simultaneously breaking Uke's balance forward to the right front corner.

Tori As you drop onto your back, simultaneously apply the top of your right foot to the back of Uke's left thigh.

Tori Throw Uke directly forward with speed and force.

54

Tani-otoshi (Valley Drop)

Tori Break your opponent's balance back-wards to his right back corner as you simultaneously advance your left foot forward.

Tori Draw up your right foot.

Tori Slide your left leg behind Uke's feet, as you attack Uke's balance backwards and drop onto your side.

Tori Throw Uke backwards to the right back corner.

55

Hane-makikomi (Outer Winding Spring Hip)

Tori Break your opponent's balance to her right front corner as you advance your right foot forward.

Tori Make a body turning in entry for *Hane-goshi*, simultaneously winding your right arm over Uke's head.

Tori Twisting your body towards your left, throw yourself forward, winding Uke's body over yours.

Tori On impact place your right hand onto the tatami as Uke lands, maintaining close contact with your body against Uke's body.

Sukui-nage (Scooping Throw)

Uke Attempt a body turning in entry.

Tori Bends forward in preparation to seize Uke's body.

Tori Seizes Uke's right leg with the right hand and Uke's waist with the left arm.

Tori Lift Uke with both arms onto your left hip and throw Uke behind you with impetus to the left back corner.

Utsuri-goshi (Changing Hip)

Uke Attempt *Hane-goshi* to Tori's right side.

Tori Lower your hips and seize Uke around the waist with your left arm.

Tori Swing Uke upwards and onto your left hip.

Tori Twist your hips to the right, throwing Uke forward.

O-guruma (Major Wheel)

Tori Break your opponent's balance forward to her right front corner.

Tori Make a turning in entry, straightening your right leg and placing it across the front of Uke's loins.

Tori Throw Uke forward over your right leg.

Soto-makikomi (Outer Winding Throw)

Tori Break your opponent's balance forward to the right front corner and advance your right foot forward.

Tori Draw your opponent close as you make a body winding in entry and pass the right arm over Uke's head. Block Uke's right leg with your right leg.

Tori Twisting your body forward and to the left, execute a winding entry to the ground, bracing yourself with the right hand on the tatami.

Uke is whipped over your back. Maintain close body contact to Uke on impact.

Uki-otoshi (Floating Drop)

Both Uke and Tori engage in *Migi-shizentai* or right natural posture.

Tori Draw Uke forward one step on the right foot as you simultaneously kneel onto your left knee, breaking Uke's balance to the right front corner.

Tori Pull downwards and throw Uke in a circular motion forward.

Instruction 5

O-soto-guruma (Major Outer Wheel)

Tori Break your opponent's balance to the right back corner as you simultaneously advance your left foot forward.

Tori Straighten your right leg and sweep it against the back of Uke's legs.

Tori Throw Uke with speed and force towards the right back corner using the back of your right thigh as a fulcrum.

Uki-waza (Floating Throw)

Uke and Tori engage in right defence posture.

Tori Draw Uke forward one step on the left foot as you simultaneously move your right foot back.

Tori Throw Uke in the direction of Uke's right hand corner. Uke makes a right forward rolling breakfall, terminating in a standing up posture.

Tori Break Uke's balance to the right front corner and simultaneously slide your right foot outwards as you sacrifice yourself backwards onto the tatami.

Yoko-wakare (Side Separation)

Tori Break your opponent's balance directly forward. Advance your left foot across Uke's centre of gravity.

Maintain a strong pull downwards and simultaneously drop onto your left side onto the tatami and thrust both legs across the front of Uke's body.

Since Uke's weight is committed forward, Uke's only escape is to make a forward breakfall, terminating in a standing up posture.

Yoko-guruma (Side Wheel)

Engage in right natural posture.
Uke Attempts an attack and assumes a posture in which the right arm is around Tori's shoulders and Uke is bending forward.

Tori Seize the opportunity to apply *Yoko-guruma* by inserting the right leg deeply between Uke's legs and sacrificing yourself onto the side.

Tori Block Uke's right ankle with the inside of your left knee and apply a strong pull downwards towards your left shoulder.

Uke makes a forward rolling breakfall terminating in a standing up posture.

Ushiro-goshi (Rear Loin)

Uke Attacks Tori with a loin technique.

Tori Lower your hips and encircle Uke's waist with both arms.

Tori Lift Uke upwards as high as you can, then remove the lower half of your body backwards and drop Uke down to the tatami.

Ura-nage (Rear Throw)

Uke Attempts a right side technique in which Uke's right arm is around Tori's shoulders and right leg is in the centre of his feet.
Tori Place your left arm around Uke's waist and your right hand against Uke's abdomen.

Tori Throw yourself directly backwards, throwing Uke straight forward over your head.

Uke executes a forward rolling breakfall terminating lying down.

Sumi-otoshi (Corner Drop)

Engage in right natural posture.
Tori Withdraw your right foot and draw out your opponent's left foot.

Tori Advance your left foot forward and to the outside of Uke's right foot, simultaneously breaking Uke's balance to her right back corner.

Throw Uke backwards to Uke's right back corner.

Yoko-gake (Side Body Drop)

Engage in right natural posture.

Tori Draw Uke forward one step on the right foot as you step back on the left foot and simultaneously draw Uke upwards breaking Uke's balance to his right front corner.

Tori Sweep Uke's right ankle sideways with your left foot.

Tori Maintain a strong pull downwards, simultaneously drop sideways, throwing Uke to the mat.

Throwing Techniques in Motion

Tomoe-nage

Harai-goshi

Hane-goshi

O-uchi-gari

In order to learn the forty throws of the *Gokyo-no-waza*, it is necessary to learn each technique from a stationary or standing position. When the techniques have been learned correctly, it is then necessary to practice them in motion, in order to adapt them into *randori*.

Therefore, constant practice is necessary in order to grasp the principle of each technique and successfully apply it in motion.

Renraku-waza or Combination Techniques

O-uchi-gari to *Ko-uchi-gari*

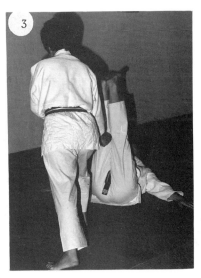

Tori Draw your opponent in a circular motion behind you to your own right back corner and attack in *O-uchi-gari*.

As Uke escapes and steps off with the left leg, follow in to *Ko-uchi-gari*, sweeping the inside of Uke's right ankle.

O-uchi-gari to *Tai-otoshi*

Tori Draw your opponent behind you in a circular motion to your own right back corner and attack in *O-uchi-gari*.

In lifting off the left leg, Uke's balance is tilted forward and Tori continues on to execute *Tai-otoshi*.

O-uchi-gari to *Uchi-mata*

Tori Draw your opponent behind you in a circular motion to your own right back corner and attack in *O-uchi-gari*.

Uke escapes by lifting off the left leg. Tori continues turning inwards, maintaining strong *kuzushi*.

Tori Throw under Uke and simultaneously sweep the right leg upwards and in between Uke's legs.

Throwing Uke forward.

Kaeshi-waza or Counter Techniques

Attack *Sasae-tsurikomi-ashi*, Counter-attack *Sasae-tsurikomi-ashi*

Uke Attack Tori for *Sasae-tsurikomi-ashi* to the right side. Tori evades by lifting the right foot upwards.

Tori Counter-attack Uke by placing the right foot down and breaking Uke's balance forward for *Sasae-tsurikomi-ashi* to Uke's right side.

Throw Uke to the right front corner.

Attack *O-soto-gari*, Counter attack *O-soto-gari*

Uke Attack Tori's right back corner for *migi O-soto-gari*.

Tori Move your left leg back and drawing Uke tightly towards you.

Tori Counter Uke with *migi O-soto-gari*, throwing Uke to the right back corner.

Attack *Harai-tsurikomi-ashi*, Counter attack, *Sasae-tsurikomi-ashi*

Uke Attack Tori by breaking Tori's balance to the direct back corner for *Harai-tsurikomi-ashi*.

Tori Step over with your right foot and move your body to your right side.

Tori Counter-attack Uke by putting the left foot up to Uke's right ankle and applying *Sasae-tsurikomi-ashi*.

Tori Throw Uke forward.

Attack *Ko-uchi-gari*, Counter-attack *Hiza-guruma*

Uke Attack Tori by sweeping Tori's left foot from the inside for *Ko-uchi-gari*.

Tori Counter-attack Uke by raising your left foot higher onto Uke's right knee for *Hiza-guruma*.

Uke is counter-thrown forward.

Attack *Seoi-nage*, Counter-attack *Hadaka-jime*

Uke Move Tori to the right front corner.

Uke Attack Tori for *Eri Seoi-nage* to the right side.

Tori counter-attacks Uke by applying *Hadaka-jime*.

The Art of Grappling

The term *Katame-waza* includes *Osae-waza*, the art of holding, *Shime-waza*, the art of strangle-holds, and *Kansetsu-waza*, the art of joint locking, whether from a lying, squatting or standing position, because *Shime-waza* and *Kansetsu-waza* can also be applied while standing.

Katame-waza is often called *Ne-waza*, which includes all techniques applicable on the ground, whether from a prone or squatting position.

Osae-waza   The Art of Holding

Kesa-gatame (Scarf Hold)

Sit in at your opponent's right side and place your right arm around your partner's neck taking a firm grip on the judogi with your right hand. Wrap your opponent's left arm firmly around your own waist and hold the judogi sleeve with the left hand. Clamp your left arm over your opponent's right arm firmly. Keep your right knee bent and close to your opponent's right shoulder. Keep your head down.

Failure to keep your head firmly down will result in giving your opponent the opportunity to counter the hold-down with a *Shime-waza* or stranglehold.

Kuzure-kesa-gatame (Broken Scarf Hold)

Sit in at your opponent's right side and place the right arm under your partner's left armpit. Keep your partner's right arm tightly under your left armpit and keep your head forward. Keep your right knee bent and close to your partner's right shoulder.

Kuzure-kesa-gatame is a variation of *Hon-kesa-gatame*.

Kata-gatame (Shoulder Hold)

Sit in at your opponent's right side and place your right arm tightly around your partner's neck gripping the jacket. Place your partner's right arm firmly across his face and hold it there with the right side of your neck. Hold the judogi with the left hand also. Keep your right knee bent.

Failure to keep the right arm tight around your opponent's neck will result in your partner attempting to escape by wedging her right arm against the side of your neck and turning inwards, ultimately breaking the hold.

Yoko-shiho-gatame (Side Locking of Four Quarters)

Take a position at the side of your opponent and place your right arm under your partner's left leg and seize his belt with your right hand. Place your left hand under your partner's neck and seize the top of his left lapel with your left hand. Draw your knees up and place your chest weight firmly down.

Mune gatame (Chest Locking) Also known as Yoko-shiho-gatame (Side Locking of Four Quarters)

Take a position at the side of your opponent and place your partner's left arm over your own left shoulder. Seize your own judogi sleeves and simultaneously draw up your knees and press your chest weight firmly down.

Tate-shiho-gatame (Longitudinal Locking of Four Quarters)

Sit astride on your opponent's chest. Place your left arm around your partner's neck and seize the judogi with your left hand. Place your partner's left arm over her face holding it firmly in position with the side of your neck. Place your right hand onto the judogi also taking a strong grip.

Kami-shiho-gatame (Locking of Upper Four Quarters)

Take a position at the top of your opponent's head. Slide both of your hands underneath your partner's arms.

Seize your opponent's belt with both hands and lower your weight down onto your partner's chest as you unset your toes and draw your knees in tightly.

Kuzure-kami-shiho-gatame (Broken Locking of Upper Four Quarters)

Take a position over the right shoulder of your opponent and grasping the belt with your left hand, pass your right arm underneath your partner's right arm.

Seize your opponent's collar with your right hand as you simultaneously lower your weight onto your partner's chest and straighten your right leg.

Ushiro-kesa-gatame (Rear Scarf Hold)

Sit in at your opponent's right side, in a reverse position and pass your left hand under your opponent's arm seizing her belt with your left hand. Wrap your opponent's right arm firmly under your right armpit and seize the gusset of her judogi with your right hand. Keep your left knee close to the opponent's body and your head down.

Kansetsu-waza The Art of Bending and Twisting the Joints

Udehishigi-juji-gatame (Cross Armlock)

 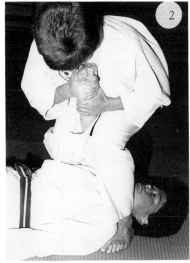 

Take a position at your opponent's right side and kneeling on the left knee with your toes set, seize your partner's right arm with both hands.

Raise yourself up on your right leg and pass the left leg over your partner's head, drawing the heel in close against your partner's throat.

Sit onto the tatami close to your partner's right shoulder and draw your partner's right arm outwards and press your knees together. Twist your partner's arm back so that the elbow joint is locked against your right thigh.

Ude-garami (Entangled Armlock)

Take a position at your opponent's side and seize your partner's left wrist with your left hand. Passing your right hand underneath your partner's left elbow, securely hold the top of your left wrist with your right hand. Apply pressure to your partner's left elbow joint by raising your right elbow until your partner signals submission by tapping with a hand or foot twice on the tatami.

Ude-garami (Straight Armlock)

Take a position at your opponent's right side and seize your partner's left arm at the wrist with your left hand. Pass your right arm under your partner's left elbow and apply pressure to his left elbow joint by raising your right elbow upwards until your partner signals submission.

Ude-garami (Reverse Arm Entanglement)

Take a position at your opponent's side and seize your partner's left arm with your right hand. Pass your left hand underneath your partner's left elbow and seize your own right wrist with the left hand. Apply pressure to your partner's left elbow joint by raising your left elbow upwards until your partner signals submission.

Udehishigi-hiza-gatame (Knee Armlock)

Place your right foot against your opponent's left knee and break her balance to the left front corner. Pull your partner onto the tatami face down.

Grip your opponent's right wrist with both hands and raise your left knee onto your partner's right elbow. Apply pressure to your partner's right elbow by pressing downwards with the knee.

Udehishigi-ude-gatame (Arm Armlock)

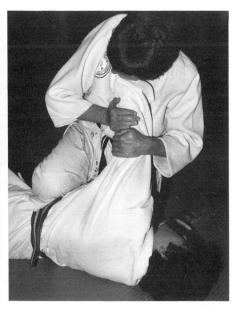

When your opponent seizes your right lapel, place both of your hands against the left elbow joint. Apply pressure to the elbow joint by twisting it around and pressing inwards simultaneously until your partner signals submission.

Udehishigi-hiza-gatame (Knee Armlock)

Sit in at your opponent's right side and wrap your right arm around your partner's neck gripping the judogi with your right hand. Place your opponent's right arm across your right knee, firmly gripping her right wrist with your left hand. Apply pressure by pressing the wrist downwards.

Failure to keep your head down when applying this armlock will give the opponent the opportunity to reach through and seize her own judogi sleeve, simultaneously barring you off with the left forearm.

Ushiro Kesa-gatame

When sitting in a position for *Ushiro-kesa-gatame* with the left arm under your opponent's left shoulders and gripping the opponent's belt with the left hand. Place your partner's right arm across your left knee holding your partner's right wrist with your right hand. Apply pressure to his right elbow joint by pressing downwards on his right wrist.

Ashi-garami (Leg Entanglement)

Tori breaks Uke's balance forward to attempt *Tomoe-nage*.

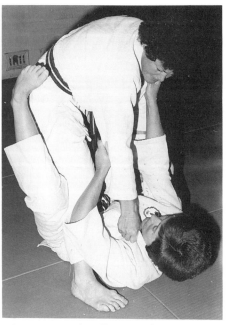

Uke resists and pulls upwards. Tori inserts her left foot around Uke's right thigh.

Tori entangles Uke's right leg, then simultaneously blocks Uke's left shin.

Uke falls forward and onto her left side, as Tori exerts pressure on Uke's right leg, causing Uke to submit with her left foot.

Shime-waza The Art of Strangleholds

Kata-juji-jime (Half Cross Lock)

Sit astride your opponent and grip your partner's left side lapel with your left hand and her right side lapel with your right hand. Apply pressure across the throat until your opponent signals submission.

Gyaku-juji-jime (Reverse Cross Lock)

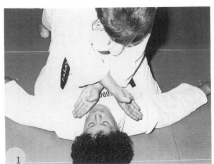

Sit astride your opponent and with both palms uppermost...

insert both hands deeply inside your opponent's lapels.

As your opponent defends herself by pushing on both of your elbows with both hands and turning her body over...

take advantage of the momentum already established and draw your opponent inwards, effectively applying Gyaku-juji-jime.

Hadaka-jime (Naked Chokelock)

Kneel on your left knee behind your opponent with the toes set, and the right foot to your partner's right side. Place your right arm under your partner's neck and clasp your hands together. Apply pressure to your opponent's throat by pulling backwards with the combined force of both hands.

Your opponent should take a firm grip on your judogi sleeve to offset the pressure of the strangle when fully applied, then submit by tapping the left foot on the tatami twice.

Kata-ha-jime (Single Wing Lock)

Okuri-eri-jime (Sliding Collar Lock)

Kneel behind your opponent on your left knee with the toes set and the right knee outside of your opponent's right knee. Place your left arm under your opponent's left armpit and seize her right lapel. Place your right arm underneath her chin and insert your right thumb deeply inside your partner's left collar. Apply pressure by choking in a wringing action.

Kneel behind your opponent on your left knee with the toes set and your right foot outside of your partner's right knee. Place your right arm underneath your partner's chin and insert your right thumb deeply inside your partner's left lapel. Place your left hand under your partner's armpit and raise his left arm up high placing the back of your hand against the back of her head. To apply pressure break your opponent's balance to her back corner as you pull with the right hand and push with the left.

Groundwork Grappling Practice

Exchange a kneeling bow to each other.

Assume a kneeling posture with the right knee up and the toes set. Both opponents take a basic grip on the judogi and try to off balance each other.

A period of several minutes is designated in which time the opponents try to immobilise, strangle, or armlock each other, while simultaneously countering and escaping.

Conclude each encounter with a kneeling bow. Change around to the next opponent.

It is very important to practise all aspects of groundwork in order to become strong, not only in holding, strangling and bonelocking, but also in escaping and counter-manoeuvring skilfully. Groundwork sessions are very strenuous and therefore develop one's endurance and stamina, particularly when practised for long sessions against strong and aggressive opponents.

Randori   Free Practice

Randori literally means free practice. When beginners first start to learn *randori*, progress is very gradual because they must first develop a basic understanding of each technique which they have learned and its practical application in *randori*. One example would be, if a beginner has just learned *Sasae-tsurikomi-ashi* in basic form, he or she would then learn to apply it when his or her

Randori Free Practice

84

partner moves in a forward direction in *randori*.

Each technique is based on a different principle and one must learn to become orientated with each technique and the decisive moment in which to apply it in *randori*. Very often, a beginner experiences the frustration of realising the right moment to apply a technique seconds after the opportunity has passed. Only continual practice in each and every training session will eventually result in success. Not only is it necessary to know the right moment and the right direction in which to apply a technique, it is also vitally important to learn the immediate evasion and counter tactic (*kaeshi-waza*) also. It is essential also to then learn how to combine techniques (*renraku-waza*), so that, once an attack has been initiated, one can continue with a combination of techniques in an attempt to eventually throw one's opponent.

One of the most vitally important aspects of *randori* is body evasions and blocking defences, because without these tactics one is continually defeated. Basic *tai-sabaki* (body turning and evasion) should be an integral part of *randori* training, from the initial stages of learning, as a beginner, and reinforced each and every training session throughout one's entire judo career.

Certain aspects can be introduced into *randori* training under a programme entitled 'Specificity of training', in which an instructor can introduce specific techniques for specific purposes, such as *ashi-waza* (foot and leg techniques) for perfection of dexterity. Some students of judo have little or no feeling whatsoever in their feet, whilst others have developed such dexterity that they can train their toes to grip the opponent's heel while sweeping. This aspect alone can take years to develop and ultimately become skilfully dexterous in.

As one progresses to a higher judo grade, one's *randori* would become progressively stronger in all aspects, such as attacking, defending, combining, countering and so forth. In some clubs

around the world many students confuse *randori* with *shiai*. A training session in *randori* is often reminiscent of a battle field, with the wounded lying around everywhere. True *randori* should still embody that basic principle of *ju*, in which the main purpose of training one's mind and body is to develop instinctive response in body evasions, yielding or giving way to strength tactics, instead of totally resisting them.

If speed, agility and body management become highly developed, then one's techniques become highly skilled, and this should become one's ultimate goal in the overall practice of *randori*.

Specificity of training on dexterity in *ashi-waza*

Mrs Betty Huxley demonstrating dexterity of the toes in *Okuri-ashi-harai*.

Shiai The Competition Aspect of Judo

Shiai is the competition aspect of judo. Many judoka love this aspect and only practise judo for the thrill of trying to win. It is important to develop *shiai* skills through constant practice with as many training partners as possible. When a judoka develops strong potential, he or she is usually entered in the State, or national selections. The winners of these events are then put into a highly specialised training squad and prepared for international, or Olympic events.

This is where the role of an instructor is converted to the specialised field of being a judo coach. An instructor deals with the technical knowledge of teaching judo from the beginning stages through to Black Belt degree and beyond. By contrast, the coach is given a group of judoka who have been selected to represent their country in a special event, and it is the specialised skills of the coach which will bring this group up to the highest standard in the shortest possible time. A good coach will determine the potential of each individual member of the squad and keep a personal record of each judoka's progress.

 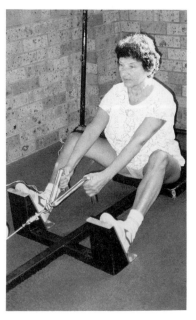

It is essential to supplement one's training with a consistent weight training programme to develop any areas of weakness.

Basic Information

(a) Name. Address. Phone number
(b) Date of Birth
(c) Height
(d) Weight
(e) Pulse rate at rest
(f) Blood pressure at rest
(g) Psychological characteristics
(h) Any current training problems
(i) Any medication taken
(j) Smoker or non-smoker
(k) Drinker or non-drinker
(l) Any other personal habits which could be detrimental to training progress

Each coach is given a deadline, that is to say, how many weeks or months are needed to get this squad into top form for the forthcoming event, therefore, a personal assessment of each judoka's physical fitness is made and a programme outlined. The coach will spend a great deal of time with this squad to ensure that their personal training chores are done correctly and increased slightly every day.

When a group first commence their programme, the training chores are set to a minimum level, according to the degree of fitness. A daily check is recorded. Both coach and judoka must contribute wholeheartedly, otherwise success will not be assured.

Bicycle Ergometer

Training daily on the bicycle ergometer will improve one's cardio-respiratory (heart–lung) capacity very much, as will running, swimming, skipping and various other activities.

Weight training will increase one's muscle bulk and strength and will provide power for heavy *shiai* training. Keep a measurement check on chest, biceps, and neck to monitor any increase in size.

Bicycle ergometer training will also strengthen the thigh muscles and the knee joints.

Specificity of Training

Speed *uchikomi* on the rack will specifically develop the following essentials,

(a) *Kuzushi*, strong pulling actions

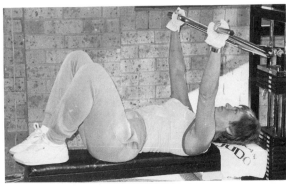

Correct supervision is essential in weight training in order to avoid muscle injury caused by incorrect lifting or breathing techniques.

Maintaining correct weight is very important prior to a special event, therefore a daily weight check is essential.

Speed *uchikomi* on the rack

(b) Speed of body turning in movements
(c) Co-ordinated foot movements at top speed
(d) Overall body co-ordination and timing.

Judoka can use a bicycle inner tube or an old judo belt. The inner tube is preferable because it will stretch and gives a quick retraction if the judoka's *kuzushi* is poor.

Co-ordinated back strengthening exercises

Overloading The judoka should train against an opponent who is heavier than his own weight category. By overloading in training, the judoka will develop endurance and should be able to cope with his own weight category more easily.

All judokas need the expertise of a coach when their standard is reaching an important level, because a good coach is also an invaluable psychological stimulus. Most Olympic teams in other sports nowadays have a team psychologist, because it has now become a recognised fact that even the most highly trained athletes have their 'down' days and their emotional problems. It takes a person with an iron will to train and be consistent in doing the daily training programme with equal enthusiasm every day.

There are many alternative ways of keeping fit which can be incorporated into a training programme. Some judoka prefer weight training, others jogging, skipping, swimming, stair climbing, rock climbing or even cross country running.

Whichever method one uses, it should be remembered that if one is not being supervised by a coach, it is important to keep a record or graph, starting at the lowest level, and carefully planning a progressive increase in the programme until the optimal maintenance level is attained. The key to success is consistency. Make a note of the objectives to be attained in your programme.

For judo, the most important are:

Muscular strength, power
Endurance
Speed, co-ordination, balance, timing
Agility, flexibility, dexterity.

The coach should note which particular techniques each judoka is especially talented in executing and encourage him or her to build a stronger range of techniques around the particular technique until the judoka is consistently successful.

Judokas must also be aware of the necessity for fluid replacement if they do not have a coach to advise them. Fluids should be replaced whenever possible. One level teaspoon of staminade in a glass of water will replace electrolyte depletion due to heavy physical exertion. It is a good idea to chew a few glucose tablets in between training breaks. Do not drink or eat heavily before training as this will adversely affect one's performance.

It is also advisable to shower after heavy training sessions and ensure that you wear a warm track suit to avoid muscle chills, especially during the winter months.

References

Sport, Exercise and You, Johnson, Updyke, Schaefer & Stolberg
Aerobics, Kenneth H. Cooper, MD
Aerobics for Women, Kenneth H. Cooper, MD
Judo Training Methods, Takahiko Ishikawa & Donn Draeger

The decisive moment of *Uchi-mata makikomi* in training.

The moment of *Hane-makikomi* in training.

Atemi-waza

Atemi-waza is the art of striking, poking, kicking, punching and cutting with the edges of the hands and feet. *Atemi-waza* is used in the practice of *kata* in pre-arranged forms of attack and defence.

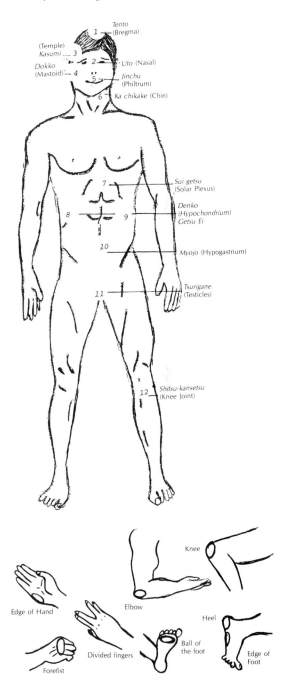

Seiryoku-zenyo Kokumin-taiiku

Seiryoku-zenyo was originated by the founder of judo, Jigoro Kano, for the purpose of demonstrating the basic principle of judo, maximum efficiency in the use of one mental's and physical energy.

The purpose in constantly practising these exercises is to harmoniously develop a well balanced and co-ordinated body by strengthening all of the body muscles.

Part One *Tandoku-renshu*
Solo Exercises

Tandoku-renshu is performed on one's own and is a series of *Atemi-waza*, or hitting and kicking exercises.

1. *Goho-ate* (Blows to the Five Directions)
2. *O-goho-ate* (Major Blows to the Five Directions)
3. *Goho-geri* (Kicking in Five Directions)
4. *Kagami-migaki* (Mirror Polishing)
5. *Sayu-uchi* (Simultaneous Side Blows)
6. *Zengo-tsuki* (Front and Rear Blows)
7. *Ryote-ue-tsuki* (Upwards Blow with Both Hands)
8. *O-ryote-ue-tsuki* (Major Upwards Blow with Both Hands)
9. *Sayu-kogo-shita-tsuki* (Alternate Sides Downwards Blows)
10. *Ryote-shita-tsuki* (Both Hands Downwards Blow)
11. *Naname-ue-uchi* (Diagonal Upwards Blow)
12. *Naname-shita-uchi* (Diagonal Downwards Blow)
13. *O-naname-ue-uchi* (Major Diagonal Upwards Blow)
14. *Ushiro-sumi-tsuki* (Back Corner Blow)
15. *Ushiro-uchi* (Rear Blow)
16. *Ushiro-tsuki-mae-shita-tsuki* (Rear Blow, to Front Downwards Blow)

1. *Goho-ate* (Blows to the Five Directions)

Execute a standing bow.

Step forward on the left foot, then the right.

Assume *shizentai*, fundamental natural position.

Hidari-mae-naname-ate Vertical blow to the left front corner.

Migi-ate Blow to the side with the back of the fist.

Ushiro-ate Strike to the rear with the elbow.

Mae-ate Punch directly forward.

Ue-ate Punch directly upwards.

After performing *Goho-ate* to the right side, immediately perform the same sequence to the left side.

2. *O-goho-ate* (Major Blows to the Five Directions)

O-hidari-mae-naname-ate Vertical blow to the left front corner stepping forward with the right foot.

O-migi-ate Blow to the right side, drawing the right foot in line with the left.

O-ushiro-ate Strike to the rear with the elbow as you move your right leg backwards.

O-mae-ate Punch directly forward, as you advance on your right foot.

O-ue-ate Punch directly upwards, jumping as high as you can.

Immediately on finishing *O-goho-ate* on the right side, commence the same sequence on the left side. It is vitally important to develop dexterity, timing and co-ordination on both sides.

The timing should be slow and deliberate, and each blow should have a reasonable amount of power when executed.

3. *Goho-geri* (Kicking in Five Directions)

Balance yourself on one foot, turn your toes up so that the ball of the foot is ready to kick.

Mae geri Kick directly forward with the ball of the right foot.

Ushiro geri Kick with the heel of your right foot directly backwards.

Hidari-mae-naname-geri Kick with the ball of the foot to the left front corner.

Without putting your right foot down, maintain your balance and draw your right heel in towards your left knee, turning your toes upwards.

Migi-mae-naname-geri Kick with the ball of your foot towards the right front corner.

Taka geri Kick with the ball of the right foot directly forward, as high as you can.

When you have completed the right side of this sequence, immediately commence the left side.

Balance and dexterity is very important in this sequence and, finally, you must develop power in each kicking technique.

4. *Kagami-migaki* (Mirror Polishing)

Kagami-migaki Commence moving your hands, drawing a circle clockwise with your right hand and counter-clockwise with your left hand simultaneously, with the right hand inside the left. This movement is executed slowly twice. The second time, the left hand should be in front of the right. Then reverse the circular movements, slowly, twice.

5. *Sayu-uchi* (Simultaneous Side Blows)

Commencing with the right fist over the top of the left, execute blows to the direct sides simultaneously, then repeat once again. Commence again with the left fist over the top of the right, executing simultaneous side blows, then repeat.

6. *Zengo-tsuki* (Front and Rear Blows)

Draw both fists in to your sides, with the thumbs facing down in preparation for punching forward.

Punch directly forward with both fists simultaneously.

After punching directly forward with both fists, turn your arms over and open both fists, so that the palms are uppermost.

Strike backwards with both elbows simultaneously. The hands remain open. Then repeat this sequence.

7. *Ryote-ue-tsuki* (Upwards Blow with Both Hands)

Strike directly upwards with both fists simultaneously. Repeat.

8. *O-ryote-ue-tsuki* (Major Upwards Blow with Both Hands)

Strike directly upwards with both fists, simultaneously leaping as high as you can. Repeat.

9. *Sayu-kogo-shita-tsuki* (Alternate Side Downwards Blows)

Strike directly downwards with your right fist, simultaneously raising your left fist.

Strike directly downwards with your left fist, simultaneously raising your right fist. Repeat this sequence.

10. *Ryote-shita-tsuki* (Both Hands Downwards Blow)

Draw both fists upwards and in to your sides in preparation to strike downwards.

Squat downwards and simultaneously punch downwards with both fists. Repeat.

11. *Naname-ue-uchi* (Diagonal Upwards Blow)

12. *Naname-shita-uchi* (Diagonal Downwards Blow)

13. *O-naname-ue-uchi* (Major Diagonal Upwards Blow)

Strike diagonally upwards with the edge of the right hand, then to the left side. Repeat this sequence.

Strike diagonally downwards with the edge of the right hand, then execute this movement to the left. Repeat both movements.

Strike behind and upwards with the cutting edge of the right hand, then execute this movement to the left side. Repeat.

14. *Ushiro-sumi-tsuki* (Back Corner Blow)

Raise your right fist to your temple in preparation to strike around backwards.

Twist your body around to your left back corner and strike with the right fist. Execute the same technique to your right back corner. Repeat once again.

15. *Ushiro-uchi* (Rear Blow)

Raise your right fist to your forehead ready to strike backwards with the back of your right fist.

Twist your body around to your right back corner and execute a blow with the back of your right fist. Execute the same movement to your left back corner. Repeat.

16. *Ushiro-tsuki-mae-shita-tsuki* (Rear Blow to Front Downwards Blow)

Stretch backwards and punch with both fists over your shoulders.

Bend completely forward and punch with both fists downwards. Repeat once again.

Step backwards with the right foot and then draw the left foot into position with the feet closed and heels together.

Execute a standing bow to conclude part one of *Tandoku-renshu.*

Part Two
Sotai-renshu   Dual Practice
Kime-shiki   (Forms of Decision)

Kime-shiki (Forms of Decision) was devised by the founder of judo, Jigoro Kano, Shihan, in 1929.

The purpose of practising *Kime-shiki* (Forms of Decision) is to teach the *joshi* judo student to make split second decisions when attacked with the bare hands, the dagger, or sword. Furthermore, to develop *tai-sabaki*, or body evasion movements, both in the kneeling postures of the first set (*Idori*), and in the standing postures of the second set (*Tachiai*).

The *joshi* judo student will ultimately be able to develop excellent body deportment, mental and physical prowess and, with continued practice, demonstrate a calm, poised attitude when controlling even the most difficult movements of defence.

Kime-shiki is composed of five kneeling and five standing techniques, as follows:

Idori   (Kneeling)
1. *Ryote-dori* (Both Wrists Seizure)
2. *Furi-hanashi* (Swing-off with Right Hand)
3. *Gyakute-dori* (Reverse Both Wrists Seizure)
5. *Tsukkake* (Stomach Punch)
5. *Kiri-kake* (Straight Cut-down at Head with a Dagger)

Tachiai   (Standing)
6. *Tsuki-age* (Uppercut)
7. *Yoko-uchi* (Blow at Left Temple)
8. *Ushiro-dori* (Shoulder Seizure from Behind)
9. *Naname-tsuki* (Oblique Thrust at Left Neck with a Dagger)
10. *Kiri-oroshi* (Straight Cut-down with a Sword)

Essential Weapons
In *Kime-shiki* (Forms of Decision), the weapons used are a *bokken* and dagger. The *bokken* is a

Miss Pat Harrington and Miss Sandra McCuish demonstrating *Kime-shiki*, Forms of Decision.

cherrywood replica of a samurai sword (*katana*), and the dagger is a cherrywood replica of the short sword (*tanto*). The correct method of handling these weapons must be learned, therefore constant practice of these forms is essential.

Both Uke (the attacker) and Tori (the defender) stand facing the official platform or *joseki*. Uke stands on the right side and Tori on the left side facing the *joseki*. Both execute a standing bow (*ritsurei*) to the *joseki*. Their distance apart is three tatami (eighteen feet, or approximately six metres).

Both Uke and Tori then turn around and face each other. Both then step in, commencing with the left foot first, then the right and stand in *shizentai*, or fundamental natural posture. Both then proceed to move towards each other, commencing with the left foot first, then the right, in succeeding steps called *ayumi-ashi*, until one tatami or six feet (two metres) apart. Both pause in *shizentai* or fundamental natural posture. Both then proceed to kneel down, on the left knee first with their toes set under, then onto their right knee with the toes also set under. Both unset their toes and sit back onto their heels, simultaneously crossing their right big toe over their left, and sitting in an upright dignified kneeling posture called *seiza*. Both then exchange a kneeling bow by sliding their hands off their thighs and onto the tatami, keeping their fingers approximately six centimetres apart and bowing their heads forward until their forehead touches their fingers. Both sit slowly upright again, drawing their hands back from the tatami and onto the tops of their thighs.

Tori remains in a kneeling upright posture, whilst Uke proceeds to collect both weapons into the left hand. Uke picks up the dagger first, placing it into the palm of the left hand, then picks up the *bokken* with the right hand and places it also into the left hand. Then levelling them off at the right side, Uke proceeds to stand up by raising

the right knee first, with the toes set, then the left with the toes also set, then coming up to a standing position in *shizentai*, or fundamental natural posture.

Carrying the weapons firmly in the right hand, Uke turns away to the right side and walking back one tatami or two metres to the edge of the tatami in normal *ayumi-ashi* movements, Uke then proceeds to kneel down onto the left knee with the toes set under, then onto the right knee, toes also turned under. Uke then unsets both sets of toes and crosses the right big toe over the left, flattening the toes and sitting back onto the heels in an upright kneeling posture. Uke then places the sword horizontally in front with the curvature inwards and the handle towards the *joseki*. Uke then places the dagger inside of the sword position, also with the tip facing away from the *joseki*.

After exchanging a kneeling bow, both Uke and Tori sit upright once again.

Uke proceeds to collect both weapons as described in the proceeding introduction.

Uke places the weapons down at the edge of the tatami as described in the proceeding introduction.

Uke returns to a position facing Tori, at one tatami and kneels down on the left knee and then the right. Both partners, using an upright kneeling posture, then proceed to draw closer to each other by sliding the right knee forward first, then drawing up the left, with knuckles on the tatami, thumbs forward. Both pause when they are one fist space apart in the centre of the tatami.

Set One   *Idori* (Kneeling Movements)

1.   *Ryote-dori* (Both Wrists Seizure)

Uke attacks Tori by seizing both wrists simultaneously.

Tori draws both wrists back and simultaneously sets both sets of toes.

Tori opens the left knee and simultaneously prepares the right knife hand.

Tori raises the right knee and the right knife hand sharply. Tori's right foot is outside of Uke's right knee. Uke responds accordingly and raises the left hand open in defence.

2. *Furi-hanashi* (Swing-off with the Right Hand)

Uke attacks Tori by seizing both wrists simultaneously.

Tori defends by drawing both wrists backwards and simultaneously setting both sets of toes.

Tori opens the left knee and prepares the right knife hand simultaneously.

Tori raises the right knee and the right knife hand simultaneously, placing the right foot outside of Uke's right knee.

Tori breaks Uke's left wrist seizure by swinging off the right hand and simultaneously pivoting on the left knee and swinging the right foot open.

Tori moves the right foot in between Uke's knees and simultaneously attempts to strike Uke to the right temple. Uke defends by seizing Tori's right wrist.

Front view of the finished movement.

3. *Gyakute-dori* (Reverse Both Wrists Seizure)

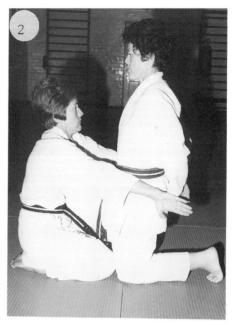

Uke attacks Tori by simultaneously seizing both of Tori's wrists in an inverted grip.

Tori defends by pulling both wrists back and simultaneously setting the toes, Tori sharply brings the right knee upwards striking Uke in the chest. Tori makes a slapping sound, clapping both hands together behind her back.

4. *Tsukkake* (Stomach Punch)

Uke raises the right fist in preparation to punch Tori to the stomach.

Uke leans forward to execute a right punch to the pit of Tori's stomach.

Tori seizes Uke's right wrist with the right hand and places an open hand block on Uke's right elbow with the left hand, while simultaneously opening the right knee up, making a body evasion movement and setting the toes of the left foot.

Tori then firmly places Uke's right wrist on top of her right thigh, whilst simultaneously maintaining pressure on Uke's right elbow.

Tori then swings the right arm over and across Uke's throat and leaning forward slightly, Tori exhales fully, applying *Hara-gatame* to Uke's right elbow and pressure against Uke's throat. Uke taps with the left hand against her own upper left thigh in a signal of submission.

Both return to a kneeling posture and pause briefly.
Uke begins to stand by raising the right knee and setting the toes, then the left, and stands up into *shizentai* posture.

Uke makes a right turn and walks in normal *ayumi-ashi* movements back to the position of the weapons (approximately one tatami or two metres).

Uke kneels down on the left knee, setting the toes, then onto the right knee also setting the toes. Unsetting the toes, Uke sits into a kneeling posture. Uke bends forward to pick up the dagger, placing four fingers of the left hand underneath and the right hand on top.

Uke holds the dagger with the tip downward and the curvature inwards. Holding firmly with the right hand, Uke takes the left hand away. Uke stands up by raising the right knee first, then the left.

Carrying the dagger at the right side, Uke makes a left turn inwards to face Tori, and walks back in *ayumi-ashi* movements, stopping at approximately half a tatami or one metre apart. Uke kneels down left, then right.

5. *Kiri-kake* (Straight Cut-down at Head with a Dagger)

Uke draws closer to Tori by sliding the right knee first, then drawing up the left until approximately one fist space apart. Uke puts the dagger down at the side of her right knee with the curvature facing inwards.

Uke then picks up the dagger with the right hand and slides it into an imaginary scabbard (the left hand), and takes the right hand away.

Uke places the right hand on the dagger handle.

Uke attacks, drawing out the dagger and simultaneously raising the right knee up, and setting the toes of the left foot.

Tori makes a ninety degree body evasion movement, bringing the right knee up, setting the toes of the left foot and seizing Uke's right wrist with an upward right grip and an open hand block with the left hand against Uke's right elbow.

Tori closes the left hand over Uke's right elbow joint while still maintaining control of the wrist and elbow.

107

After being released, Uke exchanges the grip on the dagger, by turning the tip of the blade inwards and holding it with the left hand, then regrips it with the right hand, whilst both begin to regain a kneeling posture once again.

Tori then brings her left elbow over the top of Uke's right arm and lunging slightly to the right front corner, Tori fully applies *Waki-gatame* until Uke submits by tapping her left thigh twice.

Uke and Tori return to kneeling posture. Uke holds the dagger in the right hand with the curvature up.

Uke stands by raising the right knee, and then the left knee, and returns to *shizentai* posture.

Uke makes a right ninety degree turn and walks in *ayumi-ashi* movements back to the weapon position of approximately one tatami or two metres.

As Uke finishes replacing the dagger back into position and begins to stand up...

Uke kneels down on the left knee, setting the toes under, then onto the right knee also turning the toes under. Uke unsets the toes and assumes a kneeling upright posture. Uke bends forward and places the dagger back into position.

Tori rises simultaneously. Both raise the right knee, setting the toes of the left foot, and then repeat with the left knee, and stand up in *shizentai* posture.

Uke makes a right ninety degree turn to face Tori. Walking in *ayumi-ashi* movements forward, Uke pauses at approximately half a tatami or one metre.

Set Two *Tachiai* (Standing Techniques)

6. *Tsuki-age* (Uppercut)

Uke advances the right foot forward and simultaneously punches with the right fist upwards to Tori's chin.

Tori steps back with the right foot and simultaneously seizes Uke's right wrist with the left hand.

Tori continues to push Uke's right fist back towards Uke's forehead, whilst simultaneously preparing the right fist at belt level ready for striking.

Tori executes a blow with the right fist to Uke's heart or upper chest. Both Uke and Tori then resume *shizentai* posture.

7. *Yoko-uchi* (Blow at Left Temple)

Uke advances the right foot to the centre whilst simultaneously executing a blow to Tori's left temple with the right fist.

Tori executes a left open hand block whilst simultaneously pivoting the right foot back and setting the right fist into a position ready to strike.

Tori pulls Uke off balance with the left hand whilst simultaneously executing a blow with the right fist to Uke's right temple.

Both Uke and Tori resume *shizentai* posture once again. Uke then moves around Tori for the next movement.

8. *Ushiro-dori* (Shoulder Seizure from Behind)

Uke advances the right foot outside of Tori's right foot, and wraps both arms around Tori's shoulders.

Uke demonstrates the right hand gripping the left wrist in a low position around Tori's shoulders.

Tori moves the left leg straight back and simultaneously raises both arms in a bent position with the fingers straight.

Tori then makes a transition into *jigotai* posture and moving the right arm forward with the palm uppermost prepares to strike Uke.

Tori then executes a blow to the pit of Uke's stomach with the right elbow causing Uke to completely release the grip.

Uke and Tori then face each other once again in *shizentai*, or fundamental natural posture. Uke then makes a right ninety degree turn and walks in *ayumi-ashi* movements back to the position of the weapons and kneels down on the left knee and then the right knee assuming an upright dignified kneeling posture.

9. *Naname-tsuki* (Oblique Thrust at Left Neck with a Dagger)

Uke bends forward to pick up the dagger by placing four fingers of the left hand under the handle and the right hand on top.

Pointing the tip of the dagger with the curvature uppermost, Uke begins to stand up by raising the right knee and then the left.

Whilst simultaneously executing a right turn in towards Tori, Uke conceals the dagger at the back of her right thigh.

Pausing in *shizentai* posture first, Uke then suddenly attacks Tori by advancing the right foot forward and simultaneously thrusting the dagger towards the left side of Tori's neck.

Tori makes a right body evasion movement whilst simultaneously executing a left open hand block to Uke's right elbow.

Seizing the elbow and pulling Uke off-balance with the left hand, Tori prepares to strike Uke with the right fist.

Tori executes a sharp blow to Uke's right temple with the right fist.

Tori then moves the right foot to the left and simultaneously passes the right arm underneath Uke's right arm.

Tori, maintaining strong control, steps completely behind Uke.

Tori brings Uke into the final stage of submission by pressing Uke's left shoulder backwards, and simultaneously swinging Uke's right arm high and pressing the palm of the right hand onto the back of Uke's neck.

Both Uke and Tori return to *shizentai* posture once again facing each other. Uke who still has the dagger in the right hand makes a right turn and walks in *ayumi-ashi* movements back to the position of the weapons approximately one tatami or two metres away. Kneeling down on the left knee, then onto the right knee, Uke puts the dagger back into position.

10. *Kiri-oroshi* (Straight Cut-down with a Sword)

Uke bends forward to pick up the *bokken*, placing four fingers of the left hand under the handle and the right hand on the centre of the blade.

Uke stands the *bokken* on its tip, with the curvature turned inwards.

Uke slides the right hand up to the handle and holds the *bokken* tilted forward with the right thumb on the handle guard. Uke makes an imaginary scabbard with the left hand at belt level.

Uke then places the tip of the *bokken* into the imaginary scabbard and proceeds to slide the entire length of the sword in.

Uke begins to stand by setting both sets of toes.

Uke raises the right knee up, then the left, standing into *shizentai*.

Uke makes a right turn to face Tori again, and walks forward to a distance of approximately one tatami, or two metres apart.

Placing the right hand on the handle of the *bokken*, Uke moves the left leg back in preparation to draw out the *bokken*.

Uke draws out the *bokken* with the right hand, placing the left hand on the lower end of the sword handle and closes the left foot back to *shizentai* again.

Uke raises the sword overhead and moves the right foot back.

Uke advances the right foot forward and makes a direct head cut with the sword to the top of Tori's head.

Tori makes a stepping inwards body evasion movement and simultaneously executes a left open hand block to Uke's right elbow and seizes Uke's right wrist with the right hand.

115

Front view of Tori's block and wrist seizure.

Maintaining a firm grip on Uke's right arm, Tori advances the right foot forward.

Tori pulls Uke's right wrist firmly on to the top of her right thigh and simultaneously advances the left foot in to Uke's centre. Sweeping the right arm across Uke's throat, Tori breathes out fully applying *Hara-gatame* to Uke's right elbow. Uke taps on the left thigh twice in submission.

After Tori releases Uke, Uke draws the right foot back and points the tip of the sword downwards. Both resume *shizentai* posture facing each other.

Both Uke and Tori face each other in *shizentai* as Uke draws the sword back.

Uke balances the sword in preparation for replacing it into the scabbard.

Uke then places the sword into the left hip.

Making an imaginary scabbard with the left hand, Uke prepares to draw the sword downwards.

Guiding the tip of the sword into the imaginary scabbard, Uke then pushes the entire length of the sword in.

Uke takes the right hand away and stands facing Tori, pausing for a brief moment.

Uke pushes the sword forward with the left hand, then places the right hand inside of the left.

Uke removes the sword from the left hip and carries it at the right side.

Uke makes a right turn back to face the weapons and proceeds to walk back in *ayumi-ashi* movements. Kneeling down on the left knee, toes set, then onto the right knee, toes also set, Uke unsets the toes and crosses the right big toe over the left, kneeling into an upright sitting posture and replaces the *bokken* into the correct position. Uke pauses briefly sitting completely upright. Uke then picks up the dagger with the right hand and places it into the palm of the left hand. Uke then picks up the *bokken* with the right hand and places it also into the left hand. Uke then moves both weapons into the right hand and, levelling them at Uke's right side, Uke begins to stand by setting both sets of toes and raising the right knee up, then the left, returning to *shizentai* posture.

Uke makes a right turn in to face Tori again and walks back by one tatami or two metres in *ayumi-ashi* movements, stopping at a distance of one tatami space from Uke. Both kneel down simultaneously by kneeling onto the left knee with the toes set, then onto the right knee with the toes set. Unsetting both sets of toes and flattening them, crossing the right big toe over the left, both assume a kneeling upright posture.

Uke places the *bokken* at her right side with the handle guard in line with the right knee and the curvature inwards. Then Uke places the dagger inside of the *bokken* position, with the top of the dagger in line with the handle guard of the *bokken*. Uke pauses briefly sitting completely upright.

Both Uke and Tori adjust their posture so that they sit completely upright with very dignified bearing, then exchange a kneeling bow to each other. Both Uke and Tori pause briefly, then Uke places the dagger into the left hand, then the *bokken* also into the left hand, then moving both into the right hand and levelling them at Uke's right side. Both Uke and Tori begin to stand by setting their toes, and raising the right knee first, then the left, returning to *shizentai* or fundamental natural posture. Both move their feet backwards in reverse *ayumi-ashi* movements until they have reached a distance of three tatami apart or approximately six metres. Then closing their feet together by stepping back right, then left, both stand facing each other with their feet together (heels together, toes apart). Both then turn, facing the *joseki*, and perform a standing bow.

Goshin-ho Forms of Women's Self Defence

Goshin-ho is a formal exercise or pre-arranged form of women's self-defence techniques. Originated in 1943, this kata was devised especially for women by the second president of the Kodokan Judo Institute, Nango Jiro (nephew of Jigoro Kano, Shihan).

Part one is devised to teach the female judoka to develop *tai-sabaki* (body evasion and management) movements for defence purposes, and more importantly, through continued practice, to avoid fear and panic when or if attacked.

Incorporated in part two are the escape methods for various wristholds and armlocks and the *atemi-waza* aspect of striking the adversary. In the final attack, there is a confrontation technique, where the attacker demands the lady's handbag at knifepoint. Finally, this kata should be practised sometimes with a male judoka in the role of Uke (the attacker), so that women can generally realise the importance of conserving their mental and physical energy when attacked and use skill and technique to escape, instead of fighting against superior strength. It is also important for women to use *kiai*, a loud shout, which is twofold in purpose. Firstly, the female judoka using *kiai* will find that the sound emitted sharply and with a very aggressive intonation—*eitt*—will unite the mental and physical faculties and release adrenalin into the bloodstream, preparing the mind and body for emergency. Secondly, this sharp verbal reaction shocks the attacker, psychologically shattering his ego and bad intentions.

Goshin-ho is divided into three parts.
Part One, *Tai-sabaki* (Body Management), is made up of eight movements and is practised solo.

1. *Tai-no-ido* (Body movement)
2. *Tsugi-ashi* (Following foot)
3. *Migi-sabaki*, *Hidari-sabaki* (Right movement, left movement)
4. *Migi-mae-sabaki*, *Hidari-mae-sabaki* (Right forward and left forward movement)
5. *Migi-harai*, *Hidari-harai* (Right sweep, left sweep)
6. *Migi-maware*, *Hidari-maware* (Right turn about, left turn about)
7. *Mae-shizume*, *Migi-shizume*, *Hidari-shizume* (Front sinking down, right sinking down and left sinking down)
8. *Hiza-ate* (Knee strike, right and left)

It is essential to learn these exercises before actually attempting to learn kata. These techniques consist of the basic movements of the feet in kata, such as *tsugi-ashi*, which is the traditional foot sliding movement required for all kata. There are basic body evasion movements such as the ninety degree and one hundred and eighty degree body turning movements.

These movements must be executed without losing one's balance and always maintaining body stability in motion. One must develop excellent body deportment, self-confidence and body prowess which creates a unity of mind and body co-ordinated, so that an overall alertness is always apparent.

The sinking down movements are used in rear seizure defence, therefore one must practise these movements diligently. *Atemi-waza* or striking techniques are also included for practical use in self-defence.

Part One *Tai-sabaki* (Body Movement Exercises)

1. Tai-no-ido (Body Movement)

Execute a standing bow, *ritsurei*.

Advance forward commencing with the left foot.

Assume *shizentai* or fundamental natural posture.

Advance the right foot forward one pace.

Draw up the left foot into *shizentai*.

Move the left foot back by one step.

Draw back the right foot into *shizentai*.

Slide to the right side with the right foot and draw up the left foot.

Slide the left foot back to the centre again.

Each movement is performed twice each side.

Draw the right foot in and assume *shizentai*.

2. *Tsugi-ashi* (Following Foot)

Shizentai.

Slide the right foot forward one pace and draw up the left foot behind.

121

Slide the right foot forward a second pace and draw up the left foot behind.

Slide the right foot forward a third step and draw up the left foot behind.

Slide the left foot back one pace and draw back the right foot.

Retreat back a second step by moving back the left foot and drawing back the right foot.

Retreat back a third step by moving the left foot back and drawing back the right foot.

On completing the third step back draw the right foot completely back to assume *shizentai*.

The complete sequence is executed twice to the right side first, then twice to the left side.

3. *Migi-sabaki, Hidari-sabaki* (Right Movement, Left Movement)

Pivot the right foot around ninety degrees and focus forward.

From this position pivot the right foot forward by ninety degrees back to *shizentai*.

Pivot the left foot around ninety degrees and focus forward.

From this position pivot the left foot forward by ninety degrees back to *shizentai*.

Perform this movement twice to the right side, then twice to the left side.

4. *Migi-mae-sabaki, Hidari-mae-sabaki* (Right Movement, Left Movement)

Step around ninety degrees to the right with the right foot.

Draw around the left foot and assume *shizentai*. Step back with the left foot and draw the right foot back to *shizentai*.

Perform this movement twice to the right side, then twice to the left side.

5. *Migi-harai, Hidari-harai* (Right Sweep, Left Sweep)

Advance your left foot forward and raise your right hand upwards.

Step forward with the right foot and begin sweeping your right arm downwards.

Continue the sweeping action of the right arm.

Complete the sweeping action of the right arm.

Perform this technique twice to the right side, then twice to the left side.

124

6. Migi-maware, *Hidari-maware* (Right Turn About, Left Turn About)

Pivot your right foot around by one hundred and eighty degrees to the right.

Reverse pivoting movement.

Reverse pivoting movement.

Reverse pivot complete into *shizentai*. From this position pivot by one hundred and eight degrees back to *shizentai* forward.

Perform this movement twice to the right side, then twice to the left side.

7. *Mae-shizume, Migi-shizume, Hidari-shizume* (Front Sinking Down, Right Sinking Down and Left Sinking Down)

Take your left leg back and raise both arms up to shoulder level, sinking your body down forward. Perform twice.

Take your left leg back and raise both arms up to shoulder level, turning your body diagonally rightwards and sinking downwards. Perform this movement twice.

Take your right leg back and raise your arms to shoulder level, sinking your body down diagonally leftwards. Return your right foot back and make a *shizentai* posture again. Perform twice.

8. *Hiza-ate* (Knee Strike, Right and Left)

From *shizentai* posture, raise the right knee upwards and to centre with force, then lower the right foot again into *shizentai* posture. Perform twice.

From *shizentai* posture, raise the left knee upwards and to the centre with force, then lower the left foot again into *shizentai* posture. Perform twice.

To conclude, step back right foot first, then the left.

Closing the heels together, execute a standing bow, *ritsurei*.

Part Two *Ridatsu-ho* (Methods of Escape)
1. *Katate-tekubi-dori* (Single Hand Wrist Seizure)
2. *Ryote-katate-dori* (Double Hand Wrist Seizure)
3. *Shishi-gyaku-dori* (Reverse Four Finger Seizure)
4. *Ude-kakae-dori* (Arm Wrap Seizure)
5. *Ushiro-dori* (Rear Seizure)

Part Three *Seigo-ho* (Aggressive Defense Methods)
1. *Ude-gyaku-dori* (Reverse Arm Hold)
2. *Ushiro-eri-dori* (Rear Collar Seizure)
3. *Ushiro-kubi-himo-jime* (Rear Neck Rope Choke)
4. *Ushiro-dori* (Rear Seizure)
5. *Kyohaku-dori* (Frontal Threat)

Facing towards the *joseki* both Uke (the attacker) and Tori (the defender) execute a standing bow, *ritsurei*. Uke carries the dagger in the right hand, and a strangle cord concealed inside the judogi. Tori carries a handbag under the left armpit. The distance is six feet, one tatami or two metres.

Both Uke and Tori make a ninety degree turn in to face each other and with heels together they execute a standing bow, *ritsurei*. Both simultaneously turn away one hundred and eighty degrees and kneel down, first on to the left knee with toes set, then onto the right knee with toes also set, then unset their toes and kneel back into a dignified upright posture. Tori places the handbag onto the tatami in front of her and Uke places the dagger onto the tatami in front of her. Both Uke and Tori stand up by setting their toes and raising the right knee first, then the left, and resume *shizentai* posture. Both turn about to face each other and walk in *ayumi-ashi* movements to a distance of six feet, or two metres.

Part Two *Ridatsu-ho* (Methods of Escape)

From a distance of one tatami, six feet, or two metres, both Uke and Tori step in with their left foot first, then their right, pause slightly, then proceed to move together until they are standing close to each other.

1. *Katate-tekubi-dori* (Single Hand Wrist Seizure)

Uke advances the right foot forward and simultaneously seizes Tori's left wrist with the right hand.

Tori, realising that the weakness in Uke's grip is between the thumb and first finger, proceeds to twist her left hand around and sinking her weight downwards, breaks Uke's grip off her left wrist.

2. *Ryote-katate-dori* (Double Hand Wrist Seizure)

Uke advances the right foot forward and simultaneously seizes Tori's right wrist with both hands.

Tori opens the fingers of the right hand and simultaneously advances the right foot forward, sinking her weight and pressing firmly downwards.

Tori pivots back into *shizentai* and passes the right hand through and underneath Uke's grip, breaking Uke's balance forward.

Tori tilts Uke's balance even further forward by drawing the right hand across and pulling it tightly back and inwards.

Tori releases the open hand forward sharply.

Uke's grip is broken off and Uke loses balance forward.

3. *Shishi-gyaku-dori* (Reverse Four Finger Seizure)

Uke advances the right foot forward and simultaneously seizes Tori's four fingers of the left hand.

Tori tenses the fingers to avoid having them bent backwards and simultaneously steps backwards with the right foot, then the left, pulling the fingers out of Uke's grasp and keeping the arm close to the chest.

4. *Ude-kakae-dori* (Arm Wrap Seizure)

Uke walks to Tori's left side.

Wrapping both arms through and around Tori's left arm.

Uke pulls Tori to the left front corner one step. Uke and Tori advance the left foot forward simultaneously.

Tori then pivots the right foot forward and facing Uke, Tori seizes Uke's left elbow with the right hand.

Tori pulls her left forearm which is trapped under Uke's right armpit forward, breaking Uke's balance forward.

Tori pulls her left arm free whilst simultaneously pushing Uke's left elbow forward, causing Uke to advance the left foot and pivot away turning a complete circle.

Uke comes to a stop facing Tori on a diagonal angle. Tori turns away to face the front again in *shizentai*, and Uke stands behind her.

5. *Ushiro-dori* (Rear-Seizure)

Uke advances the right foot outside of Tori's right foot and wraps both arms around Tori's shoulders.

Tori moves the left leg diagonally back and executes a body sinking down movement with the arms straight and fists closed.

Tori ducks her head underneath Uke's arms and escapes from the shoulder seizure.

Tori moves the right leg back, and Uke moves the left leg back, and they finish the movement aligned to each other.

Part Three *Seigo-ho* (Aggressive Defence Methods)

Uke and Tori face each other again in *shizentai* for the beginning of Part Three.

Uke walks to a position at Tori's left side.

1. *Ude-gyaku-dori* (Reverse Arm Hold)

Uke seizes Tori's left wrist with her left hand and applies an armlock to Tori's left elbow by pressure from Uke's right arm.

Uke forces Tori to walk forward. Uke advances the left foot and Tori the right foot.

Uke continues the pressure on Tori's elbow, leading Tori forward a second step. Tori advances the left foot and Uke the right foot.

On the third step forward, Tori pivots on the right foot, turning in towards Uke to strike Uke between the eyes.

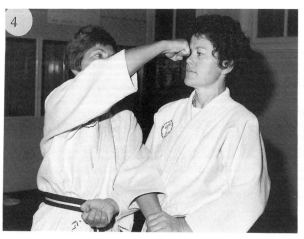

Tori executes a blow in between Uke's eyes with the right fist.

Tori seizes Uke's right fist with the right hand and pulls it sharply downwards, relieving the pressure on the left elbow.

While Uke is still holding Tori's left wrist with the left hand, Tori seizes Uke's left elbow with the right hand.

Tori draws Uke directly in front of her still maintaining pressure on the left elbow.

Tori breaks Uke's grip on her left wrist and pinning Uke's left arm tightly by her side, Tori executes an open hand slap with the right hand to Uke's right ear.

Uke and Tori walk forward simultaneously commencing on the left foot, then the right and on the third step both execute a one hundred and eighty degree pivot and face the opposite direction in *shizentai* posture.

2. *Ushiro-eri-dori* (Rear Collar Seizure)

Uke advances the right foot to centre and seizes Tori's collar with the right hand.

Tori pivots the right foot around to face Uke and simultaneously strikes Uke to the lower jaw with a right inverted fist.

Tori then pulls backwards to off-balance Uke who is still gripping the collar, and slaps Uke's right arm off with an open left hand.

Uke pivots forward on the right foot turning a complete circle and finishes facing diagonally aligned to Tori.

3. *Ushiro-kubi-himo-jime* (Rear Neck Rope Choke)

Uke takes the neck rope from the inside of her judogi.

Advancing the right foot forward, Uke slips the rope over Tori's head and attacks in a rear choke.

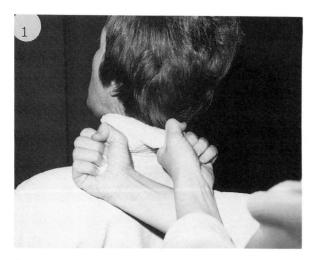

The knuckles of Uke's right hand are resting on Tori's left shoulder and Uke's left hand is tightening the choke rope.

Tori executes a right pivot in to face Uke and simultaneously strikes Uke to the chin with a right inverted fist.

Tori seizes both of Uke's elbows, applying pressure.

Tori then raises the right knee up sharply executing a blow to Uke's groin.

Tori slides both hands under Uke's armpits and steps in to Uke's centre of gravity with the right foot.

Tori pushes Uke backwards several paces. Uke still retains the choke rope in the right hand. At the completion of this movement, Uke folds up the choke rope and puts it inside her judogi again.

4. *Ushiro-dori* (Rear Seizure)

Tori faces front again in *shizentai* posture while Uke comes to a position behind Tori.

Uke advances with the right foot in line with Tori's right foot and wraps both arms around Tori's shoulders.

Tori moves the left leg back and sinks her body down raising both arms upwards with the fists closed.

Tori seizes Uke's right wrist with the left hand making a transition into *jigotai* posture and delivers a sharp blow to Uke's stomach with the right elbow.

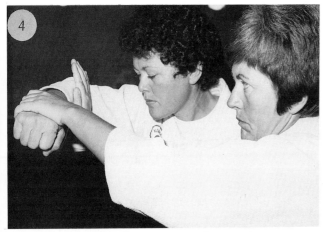

Tori then breaks Uke's balance forward, by applying pressure to Uke's right forearm with the palm of the right hand.

Uke's balance is tilted forward onto the ball of Uke's right foot.

Tori suddenly pulls downwards and withdraws her right foot backwards.

Uke is thrown forward, landing directly in front of Tori.

5. *Kyohaku-dori* (Frontal Threat)

After resuming *shizentai* facing each other, both turn away and walk back to one tatami or two metres and kneel down. Tori selects the handbag placing it under her left armpit. Uke selects the dagger concealing it inside her judogi.

Both stand up by setting their toes and raising the right knee first, then the left. Both turn to face each other and walk together, stopping at a distance of one tatami or two metres from each other.

Uke has the left hand over the knife, and slips the right hand inside the judogi, simultaneously advancing the left foot one step.

Keeping the right hand on the dagger handle inside the judogi, Uke advances the right foot a second step.

As Uke advances the left foot forward on the third step, Uke simultaneously pulls the dagger out and advances the left hand palm up, demanding Tori's handbag. Tori attempts to hand Uke the handbag and steps around by ninety degrees on the left foot.

Placing the handbag onto Uke's left hand, Tori seizes Uke's right arm at the elbow with her left hand preventing Uke from pushing the knife forward and simultaneously executes a sharp blow to Uke's face with the right fist.

Tori pulls Uke forward with the left hand which is gripping Uke's right elbow and simultaneously executes a sharp knife hand blow to Uke's right wrist successfully countering the extortion threat.

Uke picks up the dagger which has dropped onto the tatami, both move backwards until they are six feet apart or two metres. Both then step back one step with their right foot closing their left foot in, with heels together, toes apart. Both exchange a standing bow, *ritsurei*. Both then turn and face the *joseki* and perform a standing bow towards it.

'Miss Pat Harrington as Tori and Mrs Betty Huxley as Uke demonstrating *Ju-no-kata*, the Forms of Gentleness.

Ju-no-kata The Forms of Gentleness

This kata, originated by Jigoro Kano, Shihan, in 1887, is a formal demonstration of the principles of *ju* or gentleness.

This kata consists of three sets. Each set contains five *waza* or techniques, making a total of fifteen movements.

Set One

1. *Tsuki-dashi* (Hand Thrusting)
2. *Kata-oshi* (Shoulder Push)
3. *Ryote-dori* (Seizure of Both Hands)
4. *Kata-mawashi* (Shoulder Turn)
5. *Ago-oshi* (Jaw Thrusting)

Set Two

1. *Kiri-oroshi* (Direct Head Cut with a Hand Sword)
2. *Ryokata-oshi* (Pressing Down on Both Shoulders)
3. *Naname-uchi* (Nasion Strike)
4. *Katate-dori* (Single Hand Seizure from the Side)
5. *Katate-age* (Single Hand Raising)

Set Three

1. *Obi-tori* (Belt Seizure)
2. *Mune-oshi* (Chest Push)
3. *Tsuki-age* (Uppercut)
4. *Uchi-oroshi* (Direct Head Strike)
5. *Ryogan-tsuki* (Both Eyes Poke)

Ju-no-kata should be performed slowly and gracefully. Because of the grace and elegance of these movements it is generally accepted that *Ju-no-kata* is more especially suited for females, however, men also perform *Ju-no-kata*.

Uke is the attacker and Tori the defender. When a judoka practises the role of Uke, he or she is required to develop strong initiative, excellent judgement of the correct timing or movement of attack. Uke is also required to develop excellence of body deportment and graceful movements. When being lifted by Tori, Uke (the attacker) is required to develop beautiful lines of body balance and lift her feet, stretching to the highest possible point, maintaining full control.

When a judoka is practising the role of Tori (the defender), he or she is required to learn excellent *tai-sabaki* or body evasion at the exact moment of Uke's attack. Developing consistency of *tai-sabaki* will eventually lead to fluent continuity of movements culminating in the final lift or point of submission.

There are no complete throwing techniques in *Ju-no-kata*. Tori is required to prepare for the throwing technique with the correct principles of *kuzushi* (breaking balance) and *tsukuri* (positioning of the body), but there is no *kake* (throw); instead Tori is required to balance Uke at the precise point where Uke can stretch his or her body to the fullest point or extension of all body muscles. Uke then taps Tori with the free hand and Tori slowly releases Uke again. In order to let Uke reach the highest point of balance and stretch to the fullest point, Tori must perfect the lifting principles mentioned above, in order to provide stability for Uke to correctly balance upon. This requires years of constant and diligent practice to achieve perfection of every technique.

Some movements in *Ju-no-kata* culminate in positions where Tori stretches Uke backwards. It must be understood that *Ju-no-kata* incorporates stretching movements as in physical culture, specifically for developing flexibility of the shoulders and spine. Jigoro Kano introduced *Ju-no-kata* into the physical education programme for Japanese youth and it is widely practised in schools and colleges in Japan.

The syllable *ju* literally means gentle or soft and Jigoro Kano attempted to convey movements like a willow tree bending and swaying in a storm. The willow tree would escape damage in a storm because of its extreme suppleness and yielding nature, unlike the oak tree, hard and unbending, which would be smashed or damaged after a storm.

Kano Shihan's philosophy was to develop pliability of mind and body and non-resistance to an oncoming force. Tori should practise the principle of *tai-sabaki* and evade or turn away, quickly harmonising with the said force, until the opportunity arises to gain control and subdue it. Only through repeatedly facing these situations and practising the basic underlying principle, can one master the defence and attack techniques and face them with inner calm, dignity and overall body prowess. One must study the role of both Uke and Tori in order to understand both aspects

of this kata. It is essential to faithfully practise each side diligently and frequently.

If students do not understand the basic principles of throws such as *kuzushi*, *tsukuri* and *kake*, nor have a reasonable understanding of the *Gokyo-no-waza*, then they will find it difficult to study kata, as the perfection of kata relies heavily on the soundness of basic principles.

Preparation

Facing the *joseki* or official platform, Tori stands on the right and Uke on the left of the *joseki*, at a distance of three tatami, six metres or eighteen feet. With feet together and a dignified upright posture, both perform a standing bow, *ritsurei*, to the *joseki*, then pivot and face each other with heels together and perform a standing bow, *ritsurei*, towards each other.

Both Uke and Tori simultaneously step in left foot first, then right and stand in *shizentai* posture. Both then move forward towards each other, commencing with the left foot first in *ayumi-ashi* movements, or succeeding steps, until they reach a distance of one tatami, two metres or six feet apart. Both assume *shizentai*.

Set One

1. *Tsuki-dashi* (Hand Thrusting)

Uke and Tori stand facing each other in *shizentai* approximately one tatami, two metres or six feet apart.

Uke advances towards Tori, sliding the right foot forward and drawing up the left and extending the right hand to Tori's knee level.

Uke advances forward on the right foot drawing up the left in the second *tsugi-ashi* movement, with the right open hand extended towards Tori's belt level.

Uke advances forward a third step by sliding the right foot forward and drawing up the left, extending the right open hand directly between Tori's eyes.

Tori seizes Uke's right wrist with a right inverted grip and simultaneously pivots the right foot open into *shizentai*, drawing Uke forward.

143

Uke advances in front of Tori and Tori seizes Uke's left wrist with the left hand and simultaneously stretches Uke backwards, as far as possible.

Note Tori's wrist grips pertaining to the first stretching movement.

As Tori releases Uke upright again, Tori presses Uke's left wrist in by her side and raises Uke's right arm straight and both close their left foot to the right and begin turning their shoulders inwards.

Uke moves the right foot over the left, whilst Tori steps around one hundred and eighty degrees with the right foot.

Uke arches her back and stretches Tori as far backwards as possible, simultaneously taking a forward grip on both of Tori's wrists.

Uke presses Tori's right arm in by her side and raises the left arm straight. Both slide their right foot to their left, bringing their feet together.

Both turn their right shoulders inwards and pivot around into *shizentai*. Tori takes a forward grip on both of Uke's wrists and arching her back, stretches Uke as far backwards as possible.

144

Tori releases Uke upright again, then presses Uke's left hand in to Uke's left side and stretches Uke's right arm straight.

Tori slides her left hand up to Uke's left shoulder and pressing forward on it firmly, Tori simultaneously steps back, right foot, then left and stretches Uke's right arm back as far as possible. Uke taps the left hand against her left thigh in submission.

Tori releases Uke, lowering Uke's right arm and stepping inwards with the left foot, then right returning to *shizentai* posture.

Uke pivots the right foot back into *shizentai*, whilst Tori moves the left foot forward.

2. *Kata-oshi* (Shoulder Push)

Uke stands behind Tori so that her right foot is behind Tori's left heel.

Uke raises the right hand and pushes Tori on the right shoulder.

Tori bends forward giving way to Uke's push and as Uke's hand slides over Tori's shoulder, Tori seizes Uke's fingers with the right hand.

Tori moves backwards, with the right foot first, and maintaining pressure on Uke's right hand. Uke steps around with the left foot and raises her left hand with fingers divided to belt level to strike Tori in the eyes.

Tori takes several steps back and as Uke attempts to thrust into Tori's eyes with the left hand, Tori seizes Uke's left fingers with the left hand and turns Uke around.

Tori opens her feet into *shizentai* and stretches both of Uke's arms straight back as far as possible. Uke submits by moving the right heel back slightly. Tori releases Uke and simultaneously steps in, left then right, lowering Uke's arms downwards.

3. *Ryote-dori* (Seizure of Both Hands)

Tori walks around Uke's right side and turns to face Uke for the next movement. Both are standing in *shizentai* posture.

Uke seizes both of Tori's wrists. Tori pulls both wrists backwards to break Uke's balance forward.

Tori raises Uke's right arm forward, seizing Uke's right wrist with the left hand and moving the right foot across to Uke's right foot.

Pulling firmly on Uke's right arm, Tori extends her right arm over Uke's right shoulder.

Tori completely turns in and takes a strong grip on Uke's right arm with the right hand and sinking down, Tori prepares to lift Uke. Uke draws her left foot to right in preparation and places her left hand against Tori's lower back.

Tori lifts Uke as high as possible, folding Uke's right arm in against her chest. When Uke has stretched as high as possible, she taps Tori with the left hand against the lower back and Tori proceeds to lower Uke down again. As Uke touches the tatami again, she moves her right foot from her left into *shizentai* posture.

4. *Kata-mawashi* (Shoulder Turn)

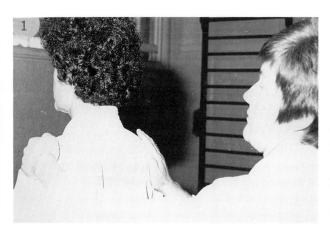

Uke pulls with the left hand on Tori's left shoulder and pushes with the right hand on Tori's right shoulder.

Uke proceeds to turn Tori around leftwards. Tori moves the right foot forward.

Tori takes an inside grip on Uke's right upper arm, breaking Uke's balance forward.

Tori enters with the right foot to Uke's right foot, then turns her body in by wrapping the right arm under Uke's right arm for the *Seoi-nage* lift. Uke brings her feet together and places her left hand on Tori's lower back in preparation for the lift.

Tori bends forward, raising Uke as high as possible, and when Uke has stretched as much as she can, Uke taps Tori with the left hand. Tori releases Uke, and when both of Uke's feet touch the tatami, Uke moves the right foot from the left into *shizentai* posture.

Both Uke and Tori pause in *shizentai* briefly.

Uke remains in *shizentai*, while Tori advances forward three steps, commencing on the left foot.

Then the right foot, in *ayumi-ashi* movements.

5. *Ago-oshi* (Jaw Thrusting)

On the third step, Tori turns sideways into *shizentai* posture, with the right side towards Uke.

Uke advances forward three movements, advancing the right foot forward and thrusting the right hand to Tori's knee level on the first step.

Uke advances the right foot forward in the second *tsugi-ashi* movement, with the right hand forward to Tori's belt level.

Uke advances the right foot forward on the third step and thrusts the right hand onto Tori's jaw. At that moment, Tori seizes Uke's right fingers with her right hand and pivots the right foot across the left.

As Tori pivots around with the right foot, Uke makes an upwards thrust with the left hand towards Tori's eyes.

Tori seizes Uke's left hand with the left hand and stretches Uke's arms upwards.

Tori draws the left foot back to the right, closing the feet together and simultaneously turns Uke over.

Tori then moves the right foot into *shizentai* as Uke swings the right foot around into *shizentai*. Tori bends Uke backwards as far as possible, folding Uke's hands behind Uke's head. Uke submits by moving the right heel slightly back in a signal of submission. Tori releases Uke and both return to *shizentai* as Tori steps inwards left, then right.

Set Two

Both Uke and Tori walk back to the centre of the tatami in *ayumi-ashi* movements commencing with the right foot.

Second step with the left foot.

On the third step, both pause in *shizentai*. Uke then turns around with the right foot to face Tori.

1. *Kiri-oroshi* (Direct Head Cut with a Hand Sword)

Uke then turns ninety degrees to the right in *shizentai* and opens the right knife hand.

Uke raises the right sword hand high with the palm turned sideways and the arm close to the head.

Uke pivots on the left foot in to face Tori.

Uke advances the right foot forward and cuts downwards towards the top of Tori's head with the right sword hand. When the sword hand passes belt level, Tori seizes it with the right hand.

Tori advances the right foot to the outside of Uke's right foot, pressing downwards on Uke's right wrist.

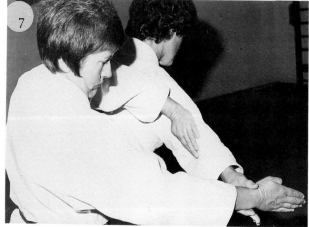

Close up view of Uke's hand releasing from Tori's right hand wrist seizure and Uke's left open hand inverted push on Tori's right elbow.

Uke gives way to the downwards pressure on her wrist and draws the right foot back into *jigotai* as Tori pushes for the second time and advances her right foot forward.

Uke pushes Tori away and Tori pivots on the left heel and turns the right foot around.

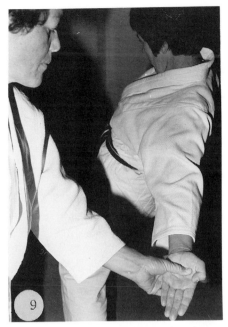

Tori passes her left hand through, taking a grip on Uke's left palm with the left hand, breaking Uke's balance to her left back corner.

Tori steps in with the left foot, then, pivoting on the right foot, swings Uke's left arm upwards, with an inverted grip on Uke's fingers and pressure to Uke's left shoulder with the right hand. Uke taps against her right thigh with the right hand and Tori slowly releases her.

Tori steps in front of Uke with the right foot assuming *shizentai*. Uke turns on the left foot and stands behind Tori in *shizentai*.

2. *Ryokata-oshi* (Pressing Down on Both Shoulders)

Uke raises both open hands to shoulder height.

Uke then continues to stretch upwards with both arms.

Uke then presses both hands downwards on both of Tori's shoulders. Tori gives way and sinks downwards, moving the left foot back into the centre and right foot across, and then pivots in to face Uke.

On turning in to face Uke, Tori's left foot is in line with Uke's right foot and Tori seizes Uke's right wrist on the outside with the left hand.

Tori draws the left foot backwards as Uke advances the right foot forward, then Tori moves the right foot to Uke's right foot.

Tori turns in towards Uke and seizes Uke's right wrist with the right hand. Uke draws the left foot in to the right and places the left hand on Tori's lower back.

Both Uke and Tori take small running steps forward for several paces, then Tori stretches with Uke as far upwards as possible as both pause.

Uke takes the left hand from Tori's lower back and at that moment, Tori makes a left turning movement pushing on Uke's chest with the left elbow and stepping with the left foot behind Uke. Uke taps with the left hand on her left thigh in submission.

After Tori releases Uke, Tori moves the left foot back into *shizentai* and Uke moves the right foot back into *shizentai*.

Both stand facing each other for the next movement.

3. *Naname-uchi* (Nasion Strike)

Uke raises the right arm across her chest and attempts to strike Tori across the nose with an open right sword hand. Tori moves her head back to avoid the blow and seizes Uke's right wrist with an inverted grip of the left hand.

Tori moves Uke's right arm away and while still holding Uke's right wrist, prepares her right hand at belt level (palm down, fingers apart) to strike Uke in both eyes.

Tori steps forward with the right foot, attempting to strike Uke to both eyes. Uke makes a ninety degree pivot on the left foot into *shizentai* while seizing Tori's right wrist with the left hand.

Tori steps forward with the left foot and seizes Uke's left wrist with the left hand. Uke then pushes on Tori's left elbow with an inverted right open hand.

Tori makes a reverse turn under Uke's right armpit and draws the right foot through into *jigotai*.

Tori completely encircles Uke's waist with the right arm and presses firmly on Uke's abdomen with the left hand. Then, pushing the abdomen forward, Tori prepares to lift Uke in an *Ura-nage* lift.

Tori arches her back and lifts Uke in an *Ura-nage* form lift. Uke's weight is resting on Tori's right shoulder. Uke submits by clapping both hands together above her head. Tori releases Uke once again.

As Uke's feet touch the tatami, Uke moves the left foot from the right to regain *shizentai* posture. Both Uke and Tori stand side by side in *shizentai* in preparation for the next movement.

4. *Katate-dori* (Single Hand Seizure from the Side)

Uke seizes Tori's right wrist with the left hand.

Tori steps forward with the right foot and simultaneously breaks off Uke's grip. Uke follows Tori by stepping forward with the right foot and pushing on Tori's right elbow with the right hand.

Tori steps back with the left foot and Uke pushes Tori's left shoulder back with the left hand as Tori simultaneously passes the left arm around Uke's waist.

Tori seizes Uke's left upper arm and begins to position her body for a left hip technique. Uke presses with the right hand on Tori's lower back and brings both feet together in preparation.

Tori executes a left lifting hip technique, balancing Uke at the highest possible point. Uke stretches, then taps Tori with the right hand in submission. Tori releases Uke down to the tatami again and Uke separates the left foot from the right into *shizentai* posture.

Both Uke and Tori walk around each other and back to a distance of one and a half tatami, approximately nine feet, in *ayumi-ashi* movements.

Both Uke and Tori pause briefly.

Both make a one hundred and eighty degree pivot and turn in to face each other, drawing up their feet into *shizentai* posture.

5. *Katate-age* (Single Hand Raising)

Both Uke and Tori take small steps forward starting with the left foot and making several little running steps in towards each other, raising their right hands high.

With their rights hands straight above their heads, both Uke and Tori almost clash together as their right shoulders touch.

Tori gives way to Uke and moves her right foot back by ninety degrees into *shizentai* and simultaneously seizes Uke's right arm with the right hand and presses Uke's left shoulder over with the left hand.

Tori then pushes Uke over to the opposite side by pushing Uke's right arm over Uke's head and supports Uke's left arm by her side with the left hand.

Tori then brings Uke upright again and slides the left hand onto Uke's left shoulder and raises Uke's right arm straight.

Tori then steps back with the right foot, then the left and stretches Uke as far back as possible, until Uke taps on her left thigh in submission. Tori releases Uke again and steps forward left, then right, lowering Uke's right arm down again.

Set Three

1. *Obi-tori* (Belt Seizure)

Uke steps forward on the left foot with the left hand above the right in an attempt to seize Tori's *obi* (belt). Tori seizes Uke's left elbow with the left hand and Uke's left wrist with the right hand.

Tori pushes Uke's left arm to the left side with the left hand. Uke gives way and slides the left foot to the left side. Tori pulls Uke on the right shoulder with the right hand turning Uke around.

Uke gives way to the pull on the right shoulder from Tori and turns forward, seizing Tori's right elbow with the left hand, as Tori pushes on her right shoulder with the right hand.

Tori steps through with the right foot as Uke withdraws the right foot into *shizentai*. Tori wraps the left arm around Uke's waist as Uke pushes Tori on the left shoulder with the left hand. Uke then pushes Tori on the right elbow with the right hand.

Tori completes the entry for a left hip technique by seizing Uke's left upper arm and wrapping Uke's arm under her right armpit. Uke does not take a grip, but leaves an open hand under Tori's armpit.

Tori begins to lift Uke as high as possible. Uke then taps with the right hand on Tori's lower back and Tori begins to release Uke downwards. Uke moves the left foot from the right into *shizentai* on touching the tatami. Both face each other once again in *shizentai* posture.

2. *Mune oshi* (Chest Push)

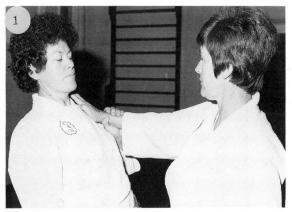

Uke attacks Tori by pushing with an open right hand onto Tori's left upper chest. Tori leans back slightly, then seizes Uke's right wrist with the left hand.

Tori then pushes Uke with an open right hand to Uke's left upper chest. Uke seizes Tori's right wrist with the left hand.

Both turn their shoulders inwards as Uke raises Tori's right arm high above their heads.

Uke steps through with the right foot and Tori with the left foot then Tori steps through with the right foot and Uke with the left, their opposite shoulders touching as Uke raises Tori's left arm above their heads.

Tori then seizes both of Uke's wrists and advances the left foot, breaking Uke's balance to her right back corner.

Tori then advances the right foot and slides her right hand down onto Uke's left elbow. Tori then pulls Uke's right arm across her left hip and bending Uke backwards applies an armlock to Uke's right arm. Uke submits by moving the right heel in submission and Tori releases Uke upright again.

3. *Tsuke-age* (Uppercut)

Uke takes the right leg backwards and the right arm back at belt level with the fingers open.

Uke then advances the right foot and simultaneously closes the right fist at belt level and, stepping in with the right foot, attempts to punch Tori upwards to the lower jaw or chin.

Tori moves her head back to avoid the blow to the chin and simultaneously caps Uke's right fist with the right hand and takes an inverted grip with the left hand on Uke's right elbow.

Tori steps forward with the left foot and turns Uke around by pushing on Uke's right elbow, then pulling on Uke's right elbow, moving Uke forward.

Tori pulls Uke forward into a diagonal *shizentai* and simultaneously draws her left foot back.

Tori changes the grip on Uke's right elbow by cupping her left inverted hand over Uke's elbow and breaking Uke's balance backwards. Tori advances her left foot.

Tori then advances the right foot forward and simultaneously passes her right arm through Uke's right arm and onto her own left forearm and pressing on Uke's right elbow, Tori bends Uke backwards as far as possible, applying pressure to Uke's right arm. Uke taps with the left hand against her left thigh in a signal of submission. Tori releases Uke to an upright position again and both resume *shizentai* posture facing each other again for the next movement.

4. *Uchi-oroshi* (Direct Head Strike)

Uke commences with an open right hand, palm facing Tori.

Uke moves her right open hand in a circular movement, anti-clockwise.

Uke continues the circular movement downwards.

As Uke's right fist passes her belt level, Uke closes her fingers into a fist.

Uke raises the right fist directly up as high as possible, with the knuckles facing forward.

Uke advances the right foot and brings the right fist downwards directly on top of Tori's head.

Tori moves her head back to avoid Uke's blow and as Uke's right fist passes belt level, Tori seizes Uke's right wrist and advances her right foot forward.

Tori advances her right foot forward in a second *tsugi-ashi* movement and Uke gives way by opening her right leg back into *jigotai* posture and placing a left open inverted hand onto Tori's right elbow.

Tori pivots on her left heel as Uke pushes her around by two hundred and seventy degrees.

Tori breaks Uke's balance backwards by seizing Uke's left wrist with the left hand and stepping in left, then right.

Tori steps into the centre of Uke's feet with the right foot and simultaneously wraps her right arm across Uke's throat and takes Uke's left arm back across her left hip holding the left wrist with the left hand.

Tori slowly lowers the weight onto her left heel pulling Uke backwards applying a strangle effectively with the right arm and an armlock with the left hand. Uke submits by tapping the heel and Tori releases Uke again. Both return to *shizentai* posture.

5. *Ryogan-tsuki* (Both Eyes Poke)

Uke raises the right hand to belt level and divides the fingers in preparation to attack Tori.

As Uke attacks Tori to both eyes with the right hand, Tori pivots the left foot back into *shizentai* and seizes Uke's right wrist with the left hand.

Uke seizes Tori's left wrist with the left hand and steps forward with the left foot. Tori places an open right hand onto Uke's left elbow.

Tori pulls on Uke's left elbow and Uke makes a two hundred and seventy degree turn around on the left foot. Tori makes an open left hand at belt level in preparation to strike Uke.

Tori advances the left foot forward and strikes at Uke's eyes with the left hand. Uke seizes Tori's left wrist on the inside with an inverted right grip.

Uke pulls Tori forward and takes the right leg back. Tori seizes Uke's right wrist with the right hand and Uke places an open hand left inverted grip onto Tori's right elbow.

166

| Tori steps forward on the right foot and Uke pushes Tori's right elbow. | Tori moves under Uke's left armpit and adjusting her feet into position, Tori wraps her left arm around Uke's waist and takes a right hand grip on Uke's left upper arm. Uke does not grip with the left hand, but draws her feet together in preparation. | Tori bends forward lifting Uke in a left hip technique. Uke taps with the right hand on Tori's back in submission and Tori releases Uke down again. Both resume *shizentai* posture. | Both Uke and Tori turn towards their respective ends and walk back in *ayumi-ashi* movements to a distance of three tatami, eighteen feet or six metres. |

Both Uke and Tori step back on the right foot and then the left closing their feet together (heels together, toes apart) and exchange a standing bow, *ritsurei*. Both then turn and face the *joseki* and make a standing bow to the *joseki*.

Miss Pat Harrington (Tori) and Miss Sandra McCuish (Uke) demonstrate the formal discipline of *Nage-no-kata*, Formal Techniques of Throwing.

Nage-no-kata Formal Techniques of Throwing

Nage-no-kata was created in 1887 by Jigoro Kano, Shihan. The *Nage-no-kata* is composed of five sets. The first set consists of *Te-waza*, or hand throwing techniques. The second set contains the *Koshi-waza*, or hip/loin techniques. The third set demonstrates the *Ashi-waza* or foot throwing techniques. The fourth set is *Ma-sutemi-waza*, the back sacrifice throwing techniques. The fifth set is *Yoko-sutemi-waza* or side sacrifice throwing techniques. Each set contains three techniques. There are fifteen techniques in all, performed left and right side.

The traditional movements in between each *waza* are called *tsugi-ashi* and are foot sliding movements in which the judoka slides one foot forward and draws up the rear foot. This is executed left and right sides respectively. There are also *ayumi-ashi* movements, which means walking with one foot succeeding the other, executed with overall body prowess. Throughout the entire kata, both Uke and Tori must display excellent deportment, dignity and bearing.

If a judoka has studied the *Go-kyo-no-waza* well, then *Nage-no-kata* will be relatively easy to learn; however, if not, then *Nage-no-kata* will be extremely difficult to learn, because excellence of technique relies heavily on the perfection of all basic *waza* or techniques. When one is required to portray Tori, one must demonstrate excellence of throwing. When one is required to be Uke, one must demonstrate excellence of *ukemi-waza* or falling techniques. To perform *Nage-no-kata* well on both sides requires years of constant study and dedication.

Set One *Te-waza* (Hand Techniques)
1. *Uki-otoshi* (Floating Drop)
2. *Seoi-nage* (Shoulder Throw)
3. *Kata-guruma* (Shoulder Wheel)

Set Two *Koshi-waza* (Hip or Loin Techniques)
1. *Uki-goshi* (Floating Hip Throw)
2. *Harai-goshi* (Sweeping Loin Throw)
3. *Tsurikomi-goshi* (Lift Pull Loin Throw)

Set Three *Ashi-waza* (Foot and Leg Techniques)
1. *Okuri-ashi-harai* (Sweeping Ankle Throw)
2. *Sasae-tsurikomi-ashi* (Propping Drawing Ankle Throw)
3. *Uchi-mata* (Inner Thigh Throw)

Set Four *Ma-sutemi-waza* (Back Sacrifice Techniques)
1. *Tomoe-nage* (Stomach Throw)
2. *Ura-nage* (Rear Throw)
3. *Sumi-gaeshi* (Corner Throw)

Set Five *Yoko-sutemi-waza* (Side Sacrifice Techniques)
1. *Yoko-gake* (Side Body Drop)
2. *Yoko-guruma* (Side Wheel)
3. *Uki-waza* (Floating Throw)

Both Uke and Tori stand facing each other approximately three tatami, eighteen feet or six metres, apart. Tori stands on the left side facing the *joseki* and Uke on the right. They turn and face the *joseki* and perform a standing bow. Both then turn and face each other.

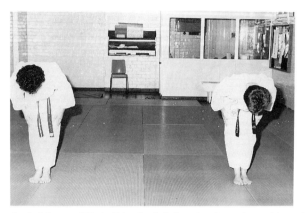 

Both Uke and Tori slide the left foot backwards and kneel down on the left knee, with the toes set, then onto the right knee with the toes set. Then both unset their toes and sit back onto their heels. Both maintain an upright dignified posture. Both perform a kneeling bow (*zarei*) to each other.

Both Uke and Tori raise the right knee, setting the toes, then the left knee, and stand up; both step forward on the left foot, then the right and take *shizentai* posture.

Uke remains in *shizentai* posture, whilst Tori walks towards her in *ayumi-ashi* movements. Tori pauses facing Uke in *shizentai* posture.

Set One

1. *Uki-otoshi* (Floating drop)

Uke seizes Tori's jacket and Tori immediately responds by drawing Uke forward on the right foot drawing up the left, whilst Tori retreats on the left foot drawing back the right.

Tori draws Uke forward a second *tsugi-ashi* movement on the right foot drawing up the left whilst Tori retreats on the left foot drawing back the right foot.

On the third *tsugi-ashi* movement forward, Tori kneels down on the left knee and draws Uke's right foot in line with the left knee, breaking Uke's balance forward.

Uke makes a forward breakfall, landing directly behind Tori.

After Uke breakfalls, both pause briefly, then stand up.

Both simultaneously walk forward in *ayumi-ashi* movements, pause in *shizentai*, then Uke turns to face Tori.

Both face each other in *shizentai*.

Both Uke and Tori engage in *hidari shizentai* as Tori draws Uke forward one step on the left foot, drawing up the right. Tori retreats on the right foot, drawing back the left in *tsugi-ashi* movements.

Tori draws Uke forward a second *tsugi-ashi* movement on the left foot drawing up the right, whilst Tori retreats on the right foot, drawing back the left.

On the third *tsugi-ashi* movement, Tori kneels down on the right knee, bringing Uke's left foot in line with her right knee, breaking Uke's balance directly forward.

Uke executes a forward breakfall.

After breakfalling, both Uke and Tori pause briefly, then both stand up and walk back several paces in *ayumi-ashi* movements, then pause. Tori stops approximately two metres behind Uke. Uke turns in to face Tori in *shizentai*.

2. *Seoi-nage* (Shoulder Throw)

1. Uke raises the right fist and advances the left foot forward.

2. Uke advances the right foot forward, bringing the right fist down on top of Tori's head. Tori executes a left open hand block to Uke's right arm and advances her right foot to Uke's right foot.

3. Tori passes her right arm under Uke's right arm and simultaneously turns her body in to complete the entry for *migi* or right side *Seoi-nage*.

4. Tori continues turning, throwing Uke directly forward.

Both Uke and Tori pause briefly after throwing. Both stand up and walk in *ayumi-ashi* movements forward. Tori stops approximately two metres behind Uke. Uke turns in to face Tori in *shizentai*.

Uke raises the left arm high and advances the right foot forward.

Uke then advances the left foot forward and brings the left fist forward to hit Tori on top of the head. Tori executes a right open hand block and advances the left foot forward to Uke's left foot.

Tori passes the left arm under Uke's left arm making a body turning in entry for *hidari* or left side *Seoi-nage*, taking a grip on Uke's judogi firmly with both hands.

Tori throws Uke completely forward.

Both Uke and Tori pause briefly. Uke then stands up and both walk forward several paces in *ayumi-ashi* movements. Uke turns in to face Tori in *shizentai*.

3. *Kata-guruma* (Shoulder Wheel)

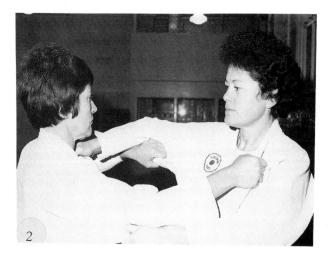

Uke initiates a right grip and Tori responds, drawing Uke forward one step on the right foot, drawing up the left, whilst Tori retreats on the left foot, drawing back the right foot.

On the second *tsugi-ashi* movement, as Tori draws Uke forward on the right foot, retreating on the left foot, Tori simultaneously changes her left hand to the inside of Uke's sleeve gusset.

Tori draws Uke forward a third step on the right foot, drawing up the left and at that moment, Tori opens the left foot into *jigotai* posture, breaking Uke's balance forward onto the ball of the right foot. Tori then bends underneath Uke and wraps the right arm around Uke's right upper thigh.

Tori straightens up, balancing Uke onto her shoulders and closing the left foot to the right.

Maintaining a strong grip on Uke's judogi, Tori then throws Uke forward.

Uke and Tori pause briefly after Uke breakfalls. Uke then stands up and both walk forward in *ayumi-ashi* movements and stop. Uke then turns in to face Tori.

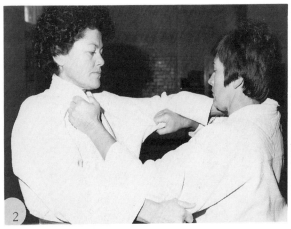

Uke grips Tori's jacket and Tori responds by drawing Uke forward on the left foot, drawing up the right, as Tori moves the right leg back, drawing back the left.

On the second *tsugi-ashi* movement in which Tori draws Uke forward on the left foot, and Tori retreats on the right foot, Tori simultaneously changes the right hand to the inside of Uke's sleeve gusset.

On the third *tsugi-ashi* movement, just as Uke's left foot comes forward, Tori opens the right foot into *jigotai* posture.

4. Pulling forward strongly with the right hand, Tori bends forward and under Uke's body wrapping the left arm around Uke's left thigh.

5. Tori straightens up, balancing Uke's weight at shoulder height and closing the right foot to the left.

6. Tori then throws Uke forward, supporting Uke's entire weight with the right hand.

7. Both pause briefly after throwing. Then Uke stands up and both turn away and walk to their respective ends.

Both Uke and Tori adjust their judogi at the conclusion of the first set, then turn to face each other in *shizentai* for the commencement of the second set. Both step forward on the left foot, then the right. Uke remains still whilst Tori walks forward, pausing at a distance of one tatami or two metres.

Set Two

1. *Uki-goshi* (Floating Hip Throw)

Uke attacks by raising the right fist and advancing the left foot.

Uke then advances the right foot, bringing the blow downwards. Tori simultaneously makes a left entry for *Uki-goshi*, by advancing the left foot and putting the left arm around Uke's waist.

Tori seizes Uke's left judogi sleeve and simultaneously completes the turning in entry for *hidari* or left *Uki-goshi*.

Tori throws Uke directly forward.

Both pause briefly after throwing. Then Uke stands up and both walk forward in *ayumi-ashi* movements. Tori stops at a distance of one tatami or two metres. Uke turns in to face Tori.

Uke raises the left arm and advances the right foot.

Uke then advances the left foot executing the left blow downwards. Tori simultaneously advances the right foot, puts the right arm around Uke's waist and completes the turning in movement for *migi*, or right side *Uki-goshi*.

Tori throws Uke directly forward.

Both Uke and Tori pause briefly after throwing. Uke then stands up and both walk forward in *ayumi-ashi* movements. Both pause, then Uke turns in to face Tori. Both stand in *shizentai* posture in preparation for the next movement.

2. *Harai-goshi* (Sweeping Loin Throw)

1

Uke takes a right grip and Tori responds by drawing Uke forward on the right foot, drawing up the left, whilst Tori retreats on the left foot, drawing back the right.

2

Tori draws Uke forward a second step in *tsugi-ashi* movement in which Uke advances the right foot, drawing up the left and Tori retreats on the left foot, drawing back the right, while simultaneously passing the right hand under Uke's left armpit.

3

Tori moves Uke forward a third step on the right foot, drawing up the left and floating Uke's balance upwards. Tori enters the right foot towards Uke's right foot.

4

Tori makes a turning in entry for *migi* or right side *Harai-goshi*, sweeping Uke forward.

5

Both pause briefly after throwing, then Uke stands up and both walk forward in *ayumi-ashi* movements, then pause in *shizentai*. Uke then turns in to face Tori for the next movement.

2. *Harai-goshi* Sweeping Loin Throw (alternative entry)

On the third step forward, Tori pivots the left foot around ninety degrees.

Maintaining balance on the left foot, Tori draws Uke's balance forward and simultaneously releases the right foot forward in preparation to sweep.

Tori then executes a sweeping upwards motion with the right leg across Uke's right thigh, throwing Uke directly forward.

Uke takes a left grip and Tori immediately responds drawing Uke forward on the left foot, drawing up the right, whilst Tori retreats on the right foot, drawing back the left.

Tori draws Uke forward a second step on the left foot, drawing up the right, as Tori retreats on the right foot, drawing back the left, and simultaneously passes the left arm underneath Uke's right armpit.

Tori draws Uke forward a third *tsugi-ashi* movement on the left foot and simultaneously enters the left foot towards Uke's left foot.

Tori executes a body turning in movement for *hidari* or left *Harai-goshi*, sweeping Uke forward.

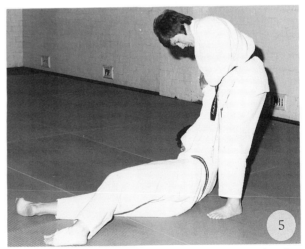

After Uke has completed the breakfall, both pause briefly. Uke then stands up and both walk forward in *ayumi-ashi* movements. Both pause, then Uke turns to face Tori in *shizentai* posture in preparation for the next movement.

3. *Tsurikomi-goshi* (Lift Pull Loin Throw)

1. Uke takes a right grip and Tori responds, drawing Uke forward on the right foot, drawing up the left, whilst Tori retreats on the left foot, drawing back the right.

2. Tori draws Uke forward a second step on the right foot, drawing up the left, whilst Tori retreats on the left foot, drawing back the right. Tori changes the right hand to a high collar grip.

3. On the third *tsugi-ashi* movement Tori draws Uke forward on the right foot and simultaneously enters her right foot to Uke's right foot.

4. Tori makes a body turning in entry for *migi* or right side *Tsurikomi-goshi*, but Uke straightens up in resistance.

5. Tori sinks down lower and Uke is thrown directly forward.

6. Both Uke and Tori pause briefly after throwing. Uke then stands and both walk forward in *ayumi-ashi* movement. Both pause, then Uke turns in to face Tori in *shizentai* posture in preparation for the next movement.

Uke takes a left grip and Tori responds by drawing Uke forward on the left foot, drawing up the right, whilst Tori retreats on the right foot, drawing back the left.

Tori draws Uke forward a second step on the left foot, drawing up the right, whilst Tori retreats on the right foot, drawing back the left and simultaneously changing the left hand to a high collar grip.

On the third *tsugi-ashi* movement forward, Tori advances the left foot towards Uke's left foot.

Tori completes the turning in entry for *hidari* or left *Tsurikomi-goshi*, but Uke straightens up in resistance.

Both Uke and Tori pause after breakfalling. Then Uke stands up. Both Uke and Tori turn away from each other and walk to their respective ends of the dojo, ending the second set.

Tori reacts to Uke's resistance by sinking lower and increasing her *kuzushi* and throws Uke directly forward.

Set Three

1. *Okuri-ashi-harai* (Sweeping Ankle Throw)

After adjusting their judogi, both Uke and Tori turn in to face each other. Tori and Uke step forward left, right. Uke remains still while Tori walks forward in *ayumi-ashi* movements until coming face to face with Uke, then both step around each other in a circular movement with the left foot.

Uke and Tori stepping around each other with the left foot.

Both Uke and Tori assume *shizentai* posture.

Uke takes a right grip on Tori's jacket and Tori immediately responds by moving Uke sideways on the left foot, drawing up the right, whilst Tori advances the right foot sideways, drawing up the left.

Tori moves Uke sideways on the left foot, drawing up the right foot at a slightly faster pace, whilst Tori steps with the right foot, drawing up the left.

3	4	5

Tori increases the pace on the third step and sweeps Uke's right foot in to the left foot with the sole of her left foot.

Tori sweeps both of Uke's feet sideways as Uke executes a breakfall.

After the throw, both Uke and Tori pause briefly. Uke then stands up and both walk forward in *ayumi-ashi* movements, then take a *shizentai* posture facing each other in preparation for the next movement.

1	2	3	4

Uke takes a left grip on the judogi and Tori immediately responds by moving Uke sideways on the right foot, drawing up the left, while Tori advances the left foot, drawing up the right.

On the second step, Tori moves Uke sideways again at a slightly faster pace as Uke advances the right foot, drawing up the left, while Tori advances the left foot, drawing up the right.

Tori increases the pace again, on the third step sweeping Uke's left foot against the right with the sole of her right foot.

Tori sweeps both of Uke's feet sideways and Uke executes a breakfall.

2. *Sasae-tsurikomi-ashi* (Propping Drawing Ankle)

1

Uke takes a right grip on Tori's judogi and Tori immediately responds by moving Uke forward on the right foot, drawing up the left, whilst Tori retreats on the left foot, drawing back the right. Repeat the same for the second movement.

2

On the third such movement, Tori turns the right heel outwards and simultaneously breaks Uke's balance forward.

3

Tori places the sole of her left foot against Uke's ankle.

4

Uke is thrown directly forward. Both Uke and Tori pause briefly after Uke has made a breakfall. Then Uke stands up and both Uke and Tori walk forward in *ayumi-ashi* movements. Both pause, then Uke turns in to face Tori in *shizentai* posture in preparation for the next movement.

Uke seizes Tori's jacket in a left grip and Tori responds by drawing Uke forward on the left foot, drawing up the right, whilst Tori retreats on the right foot, drawing back the left. Repeat the same for the second movement.

On the third step, Tori turns the heel of the left foot outwards and places the sole of the right foot against Uke's ankle.

Tori throws Uke directly forward.

Both pause after throwing. Then Uke stands up and both face each other in the centre of the tatami in *shizentai* posture for the next movement.

3. *Uchi-mata* (Inner Thigh Throw)

Both engage in *migi shizentai*.

Tori moves Uke in a forward circular movement in which Uke advances the left foot, drawing around the right, while Tori advances the left foot, drawing back the right.

Tori draws Uke around in a second circular movement by advancing the left foot and drawing back the right, while Uke advances the left foot, drawing around the right.

On the third such movement, Tori breaks Uke's balance to her right front corner and simultaneously advances the right foot to Uke's right foot.

Tori makes a right turning in entry for *migi* or right side *Uchi-mata*, sweeping her right leg upwards inside Uke's right thigh.

Uke executes a forward breakfall. Both pause after throwing, then Uke stands up and both face each other in preparation for the next movement.

Both Uke and Tori engage in *hidari shizentai*.

Tori draws Uke forward in a circular movement on the right foot, drawing around the left, whilst Tori advances the right foot, drawing around the left.

Tori draws Uke forward on the right foot, drawing up the left, whilst Tori advances the right foot drawing around the left on the second movement.

On the third such movement, Tori advances the left foot to Uke's left foot and executes a body turning in movement, simultaneously sweeping her left thigh upwards and inside Uke's left thigh.

Uke is thrown directly forward.

Both Uke and Tori pause briefly after throwing, then Uke stands up and both turn away from each other and walk to their respective ends of the dojo, marking the end of the third set.

Set Four

1. *Tomoe-nage* (Stomach Throw)

Both Uke and Tori adjust their judogi, then turn in to face each other, standing in *shizentai* posture. Both then step in with the left foot first, then the right and pause in *shizentai* once again, then both walk to the centre in *ayumi-ashi* movements until face to face with each other. Both engage in *migi shizentai* or right side posture.

Tori moves Uke backwards commencing with the right foot first. Uke retreats on the left foot.

On the second step, Tori advances the left foot and Uke retreats on the right foot.

On the third step, Tori advances the right foot and Uke retreats on the left foot.

Tori then breaks Uke's balance forward causing Uke to bring the left foot back into *shizentai*. Tori puts her left foot to Uke's centre and takes a double lapel grip.

Tori sacrifices her body backwards onto the tatami, whilst placing her right foot onto the side of Uke's lower abdomen. Uke immediately responds by advancing her right foot forward to Tori's belt level.

Uke advances her right foot forward and extends her right hand outwards in preparation to take off.

As Tori throws Uke directly over her head in a back sacrifice, Uke executes a forward rolling breakfall, supporting her own weight with both hands on the tatami.

Uke terminates standing up. Uke then turns in to face Tori and walks to the centre. Both Uke and Tori pause face to face, then engage in *hidari* or left *shizentai* posture.

Tori advances the left foot as Uke retreats with the right leg on the first movement.

On the second movement, Tori advances the right foot as Uke retreats with the left foot.

Tori advances the left foot on the third movement as Uke retreats with the right leg.

Tori changes her grip to a double lapel and simultaneously breaks Uke's balance forward. This causes Uke to bring the right foot forward to *shizentai* as Tori advances her right foot to centre.

Uke advances the left foot forward to Tori's belt level and extends her left arm forward.

Tori sacrifices her body backwards onto the tatami whilst simultaneously placing her left foot onto the right side of Uke's lower abdomen. Uke reacts by immediately advancing her left foot forward, in preparation for breakfalling forward.

As Tori throws Uke directly over her head in a back sacrifice technique, Uke executes a forward rolling breakfall, supporting her weight with both hands on the tatami.

After breakfalling, terminating in a standing position, Uke pauses briefly, then Tori stands up and walks forward, pausing at a distance of one tatami or approximately two metres. Uke then turns to face Tori in *shizentai* posture.

195

2. *Ura-nage* (Rear Throw)

1

Uke attacks Tori by raising the right fist high in the air and advancing the left foot.

2

Uke advances the right foot bringing the right fist downwards towards the top of Tori's head. Tori advances the left foot, placing the left arm around Uke's waist and the right hand on Uke's lower abdomen.

3

Tori then brings the right foot forward into *jigotai* posture and pressing with the right hand on the lower abdomen and pulling with the left arm around the waist, Tori breaks Uke's balance forward.

4

Tori sacrifices herself backwards onto the tatami throwing Uke directly over her head. Uke advances her right arm forward executing a forward rolling breakfall.

5

Uke terminates in a lying down position. Both Uke and Tori stand up. Uke turns in to face Tori who is standing at a distance of one tatami or approximately two metres in preparation for the next movement.

Uke raises the left fist high and advances the right foot.

Uke advances the left foot and simultaneously brings the left fist down towards the top of Tori's head. Tori advances the right foot and places the right arm around Uke's waist and the left hand flat on Uke's lower abdomen.

Tori then closes the left foot into *jigotai* posture and pressing firmly with the left hand on Uke's lower abdomen and pulling forward with the right arm around Uke's waist, Tori breaks Uke's balance forward.

Tori sacrifices herself backwards onto the tatami throwing Uke directly forward. Uke advances her left arm and executes a left forward rolling breakfall.

Uke terminates in a lying down posture. Both Uke and Tori pause briefly after throwing, then both stand up. Uke turns in to face Tori in *shizentai* posture. Tori then walks forward coming face to face with Uke.

3. *Sumi-gaeshi* (Corner Throw)

Both Uke and Tori engage in *migi jigotai* posture.

Tori draws Uke forward on the left foot in a semi-circular movement, while simultaneously retreating on the right foot.

Tori draws Uke forward a second semi-circular movement on the right foot, whilst simultaneously retreating on the left foot and drawing it into the centre. Tori then raises the right heel in preparation.

Breaking Uke's balance forward Tori prepares to sacrifice backwards, simultaneously hooking the right foot on the inside of Uke's upper left thigh.

Tori sacrifices backwards onto the tatami throwing Uke directly over her head. Uke advances the right foot to Tori's belt level and extends the right arm in preparation for executing a forward rolling breakfall.

Uke makes a forward rolling breakfall terminating in a standing position. Both Uke and Tori pause briefly after throwing, then Tori stands up, turns in to Uke and walks forward. Uke turns in to face Tori.

Both Uke and Tori engage in *hidari shizentai*.

Tori draws Uke forward on the right foot in a semi-circular movement, while retreating on the left foot.

Tori draws Uke forward a second step on the left foot and moves the right foot back and into the centre, while raising the left heel in preparation for hooking.

Tori sacrifices directly backwards onto the tatami, while hooking her left foot inside Uke's upper right thigh, breaking Uke's balance directly forward. Uke immediately advances the left foot to Tori's belt level and prepares to move her left hand out from under Tori's right armpit and extend it forward.

Tori breaks Uke's balance directly forward and Uke prepares to execute a forward rolling breakfall.

Tori throws Uke directly over her head and Uke executes a forward rolling breakfall.

Uke executes a left forward rolling breakfall terminating in a standing position. Uke and Tori pause briefly after throwing, then Tori stands up.

Both adjust their judogi as the fourth set concludes. Both then turn in towards each other, then step forward left foot, then right, in preparation for the beginning of the fifth set. Tori walks forward until face to face wth Uke.

Set Five

1. *Yoko-gake* (Side Body Drop)

Uke seizes Tori's jacket in a right grip and Tori immediately responds by drawing Uke forward on the right foot, drawing up the left, whilst Tori retreats on the left foot, drawing back the right.

Tori draws Uke forward a second *tsugi-ashi* movement on the right foot, drawing up the left, whilst Tori retreats on the left foot, drawing back the right. Tori pulls Uke's right side inwards with her left hand grip.

On the third count, Tori sweeps Uke's right foot sideways with the sole of her left foot.

Maintaining strong *kuzushi* with both hands, Tori sacrifices herself onto the left, side, throwing Uke directly down to the tatami.

Both Uke and Tori pause briefly after throwing, then both stand up and walk to the next position facing each other in *shizentai*.

1. Uke seizes Tori's jacket in a left grip and Tori responds by drawing Uke forward on the left foot, drawing up the right, whilst Tori retreats on the right foot, drawing back the left.

2. Tori draws Uke forward a second *tsugi-ashi* movement on the left foot, drawing up the right, whilst Tori retreats on the right foot, drawing back the left. Tori breaks Uke's balance upwards and turns Uke's left side slightly in.

3. On the third count Tori attacks Uke's left ankle with the sole of the right foot, drawing Uke's left side inwards with strong *kuzushi* with both hands.

4. Maintaining strong *kuzushi*, Tori sacrifices onto her right side, throwing Uke down to the tatami.

5. Both Uke and Tori pause briefly after throwing, then both stand up and walk to their respective ends of the dojo for the next movement. Uke and Tori stand facing each other approximately one tatami or two metres apart.

2. *Yoko-guruma* (Side Wheel)

1

2

Uke advances the left foot, raising the right fist high.

Uke then advances the right foot bringing the right fist downwards towards the top of Tori's head. Tori steps forward on the left foot and wraps the left arm around Uke's waist and presses the right open hand on Uke's lower abdomen. Uke reacts by encircling Tori's head with the right arm.

3

4

5

Tori leans backwards breaking Uke's balance to her right front corner and simultaneously slides the right leg through Uke's legs pushing with the sole of the right foot.

Tori pushes with the right hand against Uke's lower abdomen and pulls with the left hand around Uke's waist, sacrificing herself to her own left back corner. Uke executes a right side forward rolling breakfall.

Uke terminates in a standing up posture. Tori stands up and pauses facing Uke at a distance of one tatami or two metres apart.

1 Uke advances the right foot, raising the left fist high.

2 Uke then advances the left foot, bringing the left blow downwards towards Tori's head. Tori advances the right foot and places the right arm around Uke's waist, pressing the left open hand against Uke's lower abdomen. Uke reacts by encircling Tori's head with the left arm.

3 Tori leans backwards, breaking Uke's balance to her left front corner and passes the left leg through and in between Uke's legs, catching Uke's left leg with a bent right leg.

4 Tori pushes firmly against Uke's lower abdomen with the left hand and pulls strongly with the right arm around Uke's waist, simultaneously sacrificing herself to her right back corner. Uke executes a left forward rolling breakfall.

5 Uke terminates in a standing up posture. Tori then stands up, and both walk to their respective ends of the dojo in preparation for the next movement.

3. *Uki-waza* (Floating Throw)

Both Uke and Tori engage in *migi jigotai* or right defence posture.

Tori draws Uke forward on the left foot in a semi-circular movement, while simultaneously retreating on her right foot.

Tori draws Uke forward on the second movement on the right foot, while simultaneously retreating on the left foot and drawing it inwards.

Tori then extends the left leg across in front of Uke's right shin, simultaneously breaking Uke's balance to her right front corner. Uke prepares to execute a right forward rolling breakfall by removing the right arm out from under Tori's left armpit.

Tori throws Uke to her right back corner and Uke executes a right forward rolling breakfall.

Uke terminates in a standing up posture. Both pause briefly after throwing, then Tori stands up and walks towards Uke until both come face to face.

Both Uke and Tori engage in *hidari jigotai* or left defence posture.

Tori moves Uke forward on the right foot while simultaneously retreating on the left foot in a semi-circular movement.

Tori then draws Uke forward on the left foot, while simultaneously moving the right foot backwards, then drawing it in towards the centre.

Tori breaks Uke's balance to her left front corner, then slides the right foot across in front of Uke's left shin.

Tori sacrifices herself backwards to her own right back corner as Uke executes a left forward rolling breakfall to her left front corner.

Uke terminates in a standing posture. Both Uke and Tori pause briefly after throwing, Tori stands up, then both walk to their respective ends of the dojo in conclusion of the fifth set.

Both step back on the right foot, then on the left.

Both kneel down on the left knee, then onto the right knee.

Both sit in a dignified kneeling posture, *seiza*.

Both conclude by exchanging a kneeling bow, then stand up and perform a standing bow to the *joseki*.

Katame-no-kata The Forms of Grappling

Katame-no-kata was formulated in 1887 by Jigoro Kano, Shihan.

The techniques of grappling are classified into three sets and each set contains five techniques. The first set is *Osae-waza* or holding techniques. The second set contains *Shime-waza*, strangle techniques, and the third set is *Kansetsu-waza*, joint locking techniques.

Set One

1. *Kesa-gatame* (Scarf Hold)
2. *Kata-gatame* (Shoulder Hold)
3. *Kami-shiho-gatame* (Locking of Upper Four Quarters)
4. *Yoko-shiho-gatame* (Lateral Locking of Four Quarters)
5. *Kuzure-kami-shiho-gatame* (Broken Upper Locking of Four Quarters

Set Two

1. *Kata-juji-jime* (Half Cross Chokelock)
2. *Hadaka-jime* (Naked Chokelock)
3. *Okuri-eri-jime* (Sliding Collar Chokelock)
4. *Kataha-jime* (Single Wing Chokelock)
5. *Gyaku-juji-jime* (Reverse Cross Chokelock

Set Three

1. *Ude-garami* (Entangled Armlock)
2. *Ude-hishigi-juji-gatame* (Upper Cross Armlock)
3. *Ude-hishigi-ude-gatame* (Straight Armlock)
4. *Ude-hishigi-hiza-gatame* (Knee Armlock)
5. *Ashi-garami* (Entangled Leglock)

The purpose of *Katame-no-kata* is to acquire the important points for executing techniques of grappling effectively, body manoeuvring, and mental attitude, in order to cope effectively with the opponent's attack. The discipline of maintaining excellent body deportment, while moving in a kneeling position and pausing in *taka-kyoshi-no-kamae* (kneeling posture), requires mental and physical endurance and excellent concentration. Continued practice will ensure smooth execution of movement, without jerky transitions and the ultimate perfection of these principles.

Uke and Tori stand facing each other at a distance of approximately six metres, eighteen feet, or three tatami. Tori stands on the left side and Uke on the right side of the *joseki* or official platform. Both execute a standing bow towards the *joseki*, then turn and face each other. Both go down into a kneeling posture by kneeling onto the left knee, with the toes set, then onto the right knee, with the toes also set. Both unset their toes and flatten them, sitting back onto the heels. Both pause, sitting in the upright dignified position of *seiza* or kneeling posture. Both exchange a kneeling bow, then stand up by setting the toes, raising the right knee first, then the left, finishing in *shizentai* posture. Both advance on the left foot, then on the right in *shizentai*. Both Uke and Tori kneel on the left knee with the toes set, simultaneously executing *taka-kyoshi-no-kamae*, or the high kneeling posture, then opening out the right knee and placing the right hand, palm open, on the right knee.

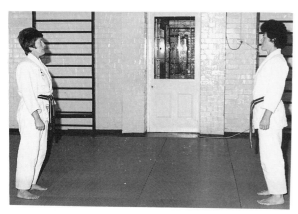

Uke advances forward one pace by sliding on the left knee, pausing, then opening out the right knee in *taka-kyoshi-no-kamae*. Uke then places the right hand onto the tatami and, pushing upwards, slides the right leg in between her right hand and left leg and finishes lying on her back with the left knee up.

Tori then closes the right knee to centre and stands up.

Tori walks diagonally across the tatami in *ayumi-ashi* movements to a position one tatami from Uke, in line with Uke's belt, for the beginning of the first movement of the first set.

Tori kneels down on the left knee and pauses in *taka-kyoshi-no-kamae* or the high kneeling posture.

Tori pauses at a distance of one tatami, two metres or six feet.

Tori then closes the right foot to centre and slides forward two paces on the left knee.

Tori pauses at a distance of approximately thirty centimetres then opens the right knee outwards again to assume the high kneeling posture.

Set One

1. *Kesa-gatame* (Scarf Hold)

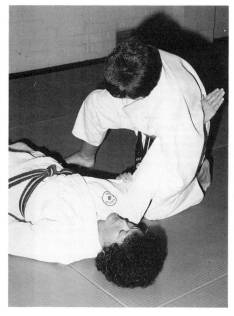

Tori then closes the right foot to centre and comes a little closer, then bends down and seizes Uke's right arm, wrapping it under the left armpit and holding Uke's right gusset with the left hand.

Tori places the right hand under Uke's left armpit and simultaneously slides the right leg through. Sitting in position on the right hip, Tori fully applies *Kesa-gatame*.

Uke tries to escape by turning inwards towards Tori and tries to turn over onto her knees. Tori counters Uke accordingly.

Uke tries to force Tori backwards by inserting her left forearm against the side of Tori's neck.

Uke makes a third attempt to escape by trying to pull Tori's left elbow forward into an armlock, while simultaneously turning her body away. Uke finally submits by tapping twice on Tori's back.

Tori moves out of the *Kesa-gatame* position and replaces Uke's right arm by her side.

Tori moves back slightly by one pace and pauses in *taka-kyoshi-no-kamae* or the high kneeling posture.

Tori then closes the right foot to centre and advances again in preparation for applying the next technique.

2. *Kata-gatame* (Shoulder Hold)

Tori bends forward picking up Uke's right arm with both hands and simultaneously kneeling with the right knee very close to Uke's right shoulder.

Maintaining pressure on Uke's right upper arm with the left hand, Tori wraps the right arm around Uke's neck gripping Uke's jacket with both hands.

Uke tries to escape by inserting the right knee underneath Tori, but Tori adjusts accordingly.

Uke tries to escape by turning inward and wedging her hands against Tori's neck in an attempt to break Tori's grasp.

Uke makes a third attempt to escape by trying a roll out over her own left shoulder. Uke finally submits by tapping Tori twice on the back.

Tori moves out of *Kata-gatame* or the Shoulder Hold, replaces Uke's right arm down onto the tatami, and moves back a little into the high kneeling posture.

Tori then closes the right foot to centre and proceeds to move backwards two paces.

Tori then pauses in *taka-kyoshi-no-kamae*, or the high kneeling posture, then closes the right foot to centre and stands up in *shizentai* posture.

Tori walks diagonally across to a position at the top of Uke's head in *ayumi-ashi* movements.

Tori kneels down on the left knee and takes the high kneeling posture at a distance of approximately two metres.

Kami-shiho-gatame (Locking of Upper Four Quarters)

Tori closes the right foot to centre and slides forward two paces, pauses in high kneeling posture, then moves in a little closer.

Tori brings the right knee onto the tatami and seizes Uke's belt with both hands, fully applying *Kami-shiho-gatame*.

Uke tries to escape by passing her left arm under Tori's head and, pulling with both hands, tries to turn Tori over.

Uke tries to insert the right knee under Tori's shoulder, but Tori adjusts the hold accordingly.

Uke tries a third method of escape in trying to turn her body over and twist out from underneath. Uke finally submits and taps Tori twice on the back and Tori releases Uke.

Tori moves out of *Kami-shiho-gatame* and slides back a little assuming high kneeling posture.

4. *Yoko-shiho-gatame* (Lateral Locking of Four Quarters)

Tori slides back two paces, then pauses in *taka-kyoshi-no-kamae* or the high kneeling posture.

Then, closing the right foot to centre, Tori stands up and walks diagonally forward to a position at Uke's right side and approximately one tatami, two metres or six feet, away.

Tori kneels down on the left knee and assumes a high kneeling posture.

Tori closes the right foot to centre, then advances two paces on the left knee, pauses, then takes the high kneeling position.

Tori then closes the right foot to centre and draws a little closer to Uke. Then, bending forward, Tori takes Uke's right arm with both hands. Tori places Uke's right arm out at right angles to Uke's body, and simultaneously slides her left knee close to Uke's right armpit.

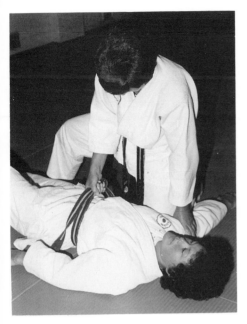

Tori places the right knee into position and taking a grip on Uke's belt with the left hand also, Tori slides the left hand down.

Tori retains a grip on Uke's right arm with the left hand, then pulls upwards on Uke's belt with the right hand.

Tori places the right arm under Uke's left leg and seizes Uke's belt with the right hand, then places the left arm under Uke's neck and seizes Uke's collar with the left hand and, simultaneously pulling with both hands, Tori lowers full chest weight onto Uke, applying *Yoko-shiho-gatame.*

Uke tries to escape by pushing Tori's head away and wrapping the left leg over Tori's head. Tori adjusts the hold accordingly.

Uke tries to escape by pushing her right elbow inside of Tori's left thigh, pushing Tori away and simultaneously turning in towards Tori. Uke then submits by tapping Tori twice.

Tori moves out of the *Yoko-shiho-gatame* position and puts Uke's right arm back into position. Tori then moves back a little and pauses in a high kneeling posture.

Tori closes the right foot to centre and moves backwards two paces, then pauses in high kneeling position.

Tori then stands up and walks diagonally back to a position at the top of Uke's head.

5. *Kuzure-kami-shiho-gatame* (Broken Upper Locking of Four Quarters)

Tori kneels down in *taka-kyoshi-no-kamae* at a distance of approximately one tatami.

Tori then closes the right foot to centre and advances two paces on the left knee. Tori pauses in high kneeling posture.

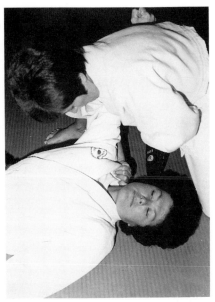

Tori then closes the right foot to centre and moves a little closer. Moving the right foot around Uke's right shoulder, Tori wraps the right arm around Uke's right arm and seizes Uke's right lapel with the right hand.

Tori lowers the right knee into position and places the left arm under Uke's left arm seizing Uke's belt. Lowering full chest weight onto Uke, Tori applies *Kuzure-kami-shiho-gatame*.

221

Uke tries to escape by turning inwards and gripping Tori's jacket in an effort to turn Tori over.

Uke bridges and pushes backwards in an effort to turn out from underneath Tori.

Uke submits by tapping Tori twice on the back and Tori releases Uke. Tori reverts to high kneeling posture.

Tori moves backwards two paces and pauses in *taka-kyoshi-no-kamae* or the high kneeling posture.

Uke presses the right hand onto the tatami and draws the right leg through the left foot and the right hand to assume *taka-kyoshi-no-kamae* or the high kneeling posture.

Both Uke and Tori adjust their judogi at the end of the first set. Both then pause in high kneeling posture.

Set Two

1. Kata-juji-jime (Half Cross Chokelock)

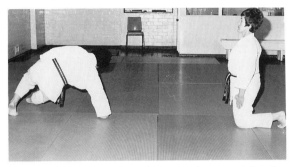

Uke then proceeds to go down to the tatami for the beginning of the second set. Placing the right hand onto the tatami and supporting her entire body weight, Uke turns the right leg through and lowers her body down to the tatami lying flat with the left knee up.

Tori brings the right foot to centre and stands up in *shizentai* posture.

Tori walks diagonally across to a position at Uke's right side, in *ayumi-ashi* movements.

Tori kneels down on the left knee in *taka-kyoshi-no-kamae* at a distance of approximately one tatami.

Tori closes the right foot to the centre then slides forward two paces and pauses in high kneeling posture.

Tori moves a little closer, then bends forward. Picking up Uke's right arm with both hands, Tori places it at right angles to Uke's body.

Tori then pushes Uke's left arm out at left angles to Uke's body with her right hand, and simultaneously moves the right leg over the top of Uke's body.

Tori seizes Uke's left lapel with the right hand, then slides the left hand deep inside the collar. Tori moves her left knee closer in.

Tori then encircles Uke's head in a flowing movement with the right hand.

Tori then seizes Uke's right lapel with the right hand and simultaneously lowers the grip on Uke's left lapel with the left hand.

Uke attempts to escape by bridging her body upwards and trying to turn. Tori applies the inside of her right forearm across Uke's throat and lowering her head down fully applies *Kata-juji-jime*. Uke submits by tapping twice on Tori's back and Tori immediately releases Uke.

Tori simultaneously moves the right leg over Uke's body, closes Uke's left arm back into position and straightens Uke's left lapel.

Tori picks Uke's arm up with both hands and places it back into position at Uke's right side.

Tori moves back a little and assumes *taka-kyoshi-no-kamae* or the high kneeling posture.

Tori then closes the right foot to centre, moves backwards two paces and assumes high kneeling posture.

Tori closes the right foot to centre.

Tori stands in *shizentai* posture, then walks diagonally forward to a position at Uke's head.

2. *Hadaka-jime* (Naked Stranglehold)

Tori kneels down on the left knee in *taka-kyoshi-no-kamae*, at a distance of approximately half a tatami or one metre.

Uke sits upright, then Tori closes the right foot to centre and advances forward two paces.

Tori pauses in *taka-kyoshi-no-kamae*.

Tori then draws a little closer and places the right foot near Uke's right hip and passes the right arm around Uke's neck, cupping the right hand into the left.

Tori moves back a little and applies *Hadaka-jime*. Uke grabs Tori's right judogi sleeve and pulls forward while submitting by tapping the right foot twice.

Tori releases Uke and moves back a little assuming *taka-kyoshi-no-kamae*, and Uke composes herself.

3. *Okuri-eri-jime* (Sliding Collar Chokelock)

Tori moves in a little, placing the right foot near Uke's right hip and the left arm under Uke's left armpit, seizing Uke's right lapel with the left hand. Tori then places the right arm around Uke's neck and takes a tight grip on Uke's left inside lapel with the right hand.

Tori lowers her head against the side of Uke's head and fully applies *Okuri-eri-jime*. Uke immediately seizes Tori's right judogi sleeve with both hands and pulls forward, while simultaneously submitting by tapping on the tatami twice with the right foot.

4. *Kataha-jime* (Single Wing Chocklock)

Tori releases Uke, then moves back a little in high kneeling posture, while Uke composes herself.

Tori advances the right foot and places the left arm under Uke's left armpit and the right arm around Uke's neck, taking a grip with the right hand inside of Uke's left lapel.

Tori places the back of her left hand (not the palm) against the nape of Uke's neck pressing the head forward, while simultaneously choking Uke with the right hand. Uke submits by tapping the right foot twice on the tatami.

Tori releases Uke and moves back a little in high kneeling posture.

5. *Gyaku-juji-jime* (Reverse Cross Chokelock)

Tori moves the right foot to centre, then moves backwards two paces and Uke simultaneously assumes a lying down posture with the left knee up.

Tori pauses in *taka-kyoshi-no-kamae*.

Tori moves the right foot to centre, then stands up in *shizentai*. Tori walks diagonally forward to a position at Uke's right side in line with Uke's belt.

Tori kneels down on the left knee in high kneeling posture at a distance of approximately one tatami, two metres or six feet.

Tori moves the right foot to centre, then slides forward two paces and pauses in high kneeling posture.

Tori draws a little closer, then bends forward and picks up Uke's right arm with both hands and places it at right angles to Uke's body, drawing the left knee in close to Uke's right armpit.

Tori seizes Uke's left lapel with the right hand, then inserts the left hand deeply inside of Uke's left collar.

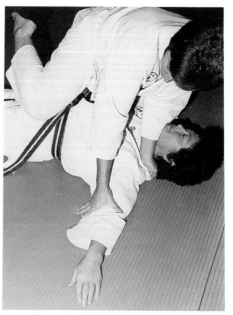

Tori then places the right hand onto Uke's left arm, and simultaneously slides the left arm out at right angles, while moving the right leg over Uke's body.

Tori encirles Uke's head with the right hand.

Tori takes an inside grip with the right hand on Uke's right inside lapel.

Uke immediately attempts to escape by holding Tori's arms at the elbow, bridging her body upwards and rolling sideways.

Tori pulls Uke's head up with both hands and rolls to her right side, pulling Uke over and on top of her.

Tori holds Uke in between her legs and, pulling firmly with both hands in towards her own chest, Tori applies *Gyaku-juji-jime*. Uke hits both hands on the tatami in submission.

Uke pushes on Tori's shoulders as Tori turns Uke on her back again.

Tori releases the grip on Uke's right lapel with the right hand and simultaneously closes Uke's left arm against Uke's left side, while passing the right leg over Uke's body.

Tori replaces Uke's right arm.

Tori moves back a little.

Tori assumes high kneeling posture.

Tori moves the right foot to centre and stands up in *shizentai*, then walks forward in *ayumi-ashi* movements.

Tori moves the right foot to centre, then slides backwards two paces and pauses in *taka-kyoshi-no-kamae* or high kneeling posture.

Tori kneels down in high kneeling posture in a position above Uke's head.

Set Three

1. Ude-garami (Entangled Armlock)

Uke pushes the right hand onto the tatami and draws the right leg through, coming up to a high kneeling posture.

Uke and Tori adjust their judogi for the conclusion of the second set. Both prepare for the beginning of the third set.

Uke extends the right hand towards the tatami in preparation to go down to the tatami.

Uke resumes a lying posture with the left knee up. Tori closes the right foot to left, stands up in *shizentai* posture and walks diagonally forward.

Tori kneels down on the left knee in high kneeling posture at a distance of one tatami or two metres.

Tori closes the right foot to centre and slides forward two paces, then takes the high kneeling position.

Tori then draws a little closer, bends forward and picks up Uke's right arm with both hands, placing it out at right angles to Uke's body. Tori brings the left knee in close to Uke's right armpit.

Uke attempts to grab Tori's right lapel with her left hand, but Tori reacts by taking an inverted grip on Uke's left wrist with the left hand and placing the right hand behind Uke's left elbow.

Tori leans forward onto Uke's chest and placing her right hand onto her own left wrist, Tori fully applies *Ude-garami*. Uke submits by tapping twice on Tori's back with the right hand. Tori immediately releases Uke and places her left hand back in position.

Tori then picks up Uke's right arm with both hands and places it back into position at Uke's right side.

2. *Ude-hishigi-juji-gatame* (Upper Cross Armlock)

Tori moves back a little, then pauses in high kneeling position. Tori then moves in a little closer.

Uke reaches up and seizes Tori's left lapel with her right hand. Tori immediately reacts by seizing Uke's right wrist with both hands and sliding the right foot under Uke's right armpit.

Tori moves the left foot over Uke's head and tightens the back of her left heel against the left side of Uke's throat, while squatting very close to Uke's right shoulder.

Tori sits back onto the tatami applying pressure to Uke's right elbow across the top of her right thigh, while bringing her knees together.

Uke taps on Tori's left leg twice in submission and Tori releases Uke and moves out of the *Ude-hishigi-juji-gatame* position into the high kneeling posture.

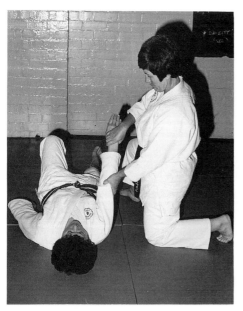

Tori then moves back a little into *taka-kyoshi-no-kamae*.

Tori then puts Uke's right arm back into position at Uke's right side.

3. *Ude-hishigi-ude-gatame* (Straight Armlock)

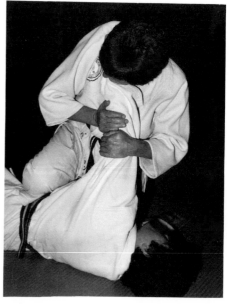

Tori moves a little closer, then bends forward picking up Uke's right arm with both hands and placing it at right angles to Uke's body, while drawing the left knee closer.

Uke tries to seize Tori's right lapel with the left hand while raising herself up. Tori immediately applies both open hands against Uke's left elbow joint and, holding Uke's left wrist with the chin, Tori pins Uke's hips with the right knee and fully applies *Ude-hishigi-ude-gatame*. Uke submits by tapping Tori with the right hand.

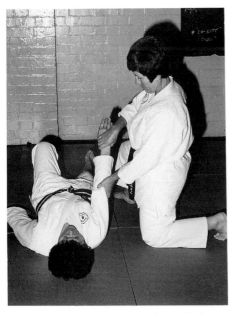

Tori moves back a little and pauses in *taka-kyoshi-no-kamae*. Tori then closes the right foot to centre and slides backwards two paces, then pauses in high kneeling position.

Tori releases Uke immediately, and places Uke's left arm back into position, then picks up Uke's right arm with both hands and places it at Uke's right side.

Tori then closes the right foot to centre, stands up in *shizentai* posture and walks forward to a position in line with Uke's head.

Tori kneels down on the left knee in *taka-kyoshi-no-kamae* at a distance of approximately half a tatami or one metre.

4. Ude-hishigi-hiza-gatame (Knee Armlock)

Uke presses the right hand onto the tatami and draws the right leg through, coming up to a high kneeling posture. From a distance of approximately one tatami or two metres, both close the right foot to centre and slide forward.

Both engage in a right kneeling posture.

Tori lets go of her left grip on Uke's right sleeve passing her left hand under Uke's right arm, then back over the top, Tori breaks off Uke's right grip on Tori's left lapel, firmly wrapping Uke's arm underneath Tori's left armpit, and simultaneously breaking Uke's balance to Uke's left front corner.

Tori places her right foot on Uke's upper left thigh.

Tori raises her left knee and places it onto Uke's right elbow joint firmly. Uke submits by tapping the left hand on the tatami. Tori releases Uke immediately.

Tori pulls Uke forward to Uke's left front corner and simultaneously pushes Uke's left knee backwards with her right foot.

5. *Ashi-garami* (Entangled Leglock)

Uke and Tori engage in *migi shizentai* or right natural posture.

Tori attempts to execute a *migi Tomoe-nage* or right side Stomach Throw, but Uke defends by lifting Tori upwards.

Tori pushes her right instep against Uke's left knee and, breaking Uke's balance to Uke's left front corner, Tori pulls Uke face downwards onto the tatami.

Tori entwines her left leg under and through Uke's right leg.

Tori pushes her left leg deeply through causing Uke to submit with the left hand on the tatami. Tori immediately releases Uke.

Both come up to a kneeling posture.

Uke moves back one pace and pauses in high kneeling posture, then Tori moves back two paces and pauses in high kneeling posture.

Both close their right foot to centre, then stand up in *shizentai* posture.

Uke and Tori step back with the right foot, then the left, closing their heels together and toes apart.

Both kneel down on the left knee with their toes set, then onto the right knee, and, unsetting their toes, both sit upright in *seiza*. Then both exchange a kneeling bow.

Both Uke and Tori raise the right knee, setting their toes, then the left, and stand up facing each other with their heels together and toes apart. Then both turn and face the *joseki* and perform a standing bow towards the *joseki* to conclude the *Katame-no-kata*.

Miss Pat Harringtron and Miss Sandra McCuish demonstrate *Kime-no-kata*, Forms of Self-Defence.

Kime-no-kata The Forms of Self-Defence

Kime-no-kata was formulated in 1887 by Jigoro Kano, Shihan. *Kime-no-kata* consists of two sets. The first set has eight movements, performed in a kneeling position. The second set contains twelve movements applicable in a standing posture. A total of twenty movements.

Set One *Idori* (Techniques Applicable in a Kneeling Posture)

Attacks with the Bare Hands
1. *Ryote-dori* (Both Wrists Seizure)
2. *Tsukkake* (Stomach Punch)
3. *Suri-age* (Thrust at the Forehead)
4. *Yoko-uchi* (Blow at the Left temple)
5. *Ushiro-dori* (Shoulder Seizure from Behind)

Attacks with the Dagger
6. *Tsukkomi* (Dagger Thrust at the Stomach)
6. *Kiri-komi* (Straight Cut-down at Head with a Dagger)
8. *Yoko-tsuki* (Side Thrust with a Dagger)

Set Two *Tachiai* (Techniques Applicable in a Standing Position

Attacks with the Bare Hands
9. *Ryote-dori* (Both Wrists Seizure)
10. *Sode-dori* (Sleeve Seizure from the Side)
11. *Tsuki-kake* (Straight Strike to the Face)
12. *Tsuki-age* (Upper-cut)
13. *Suri-age* (Thrust at the Forehead)
14. *Yoko-uchi* (Blow at the Left Temple)
15. *Keage* (Testicles Kick)
16. *Ushiro-dori* (Shoulder Seizure from Behind)

Attacks with the Dagger and Sword
17. *Tsuki-komi* (Dagger Thrust at the Stomach)
18. *Kiri-komi* (Straight Cut-down at Head with a Dagger)
19. *Nuki-kake* (Sword Unsheathing)
20. *Kiri-oroshi* (Straight Cut-down with a Sword)

When one is required to portray Tori in *Kime-no-kata*, one must be able to demonstrate excellent *tai-sabaki* or body manipulation movements. Moving one's body away from all of the attacks in this particular kata requires many years of dedicated practice and understanding of the correct principles.

In *Kime-no-kata*, Tori is attacked with the bare hands, both in the kneeling posture and the standing posture in a variety of different ways. Tori is also attacked with the short and long swords, which are actually cherrywood replicas of the *tanto* or short sword, and the *katana* or long sword.

Tori must also learn to develop *kime* or 'focus' and also controlled breathing, and must never leave herself off guard at any time. Eternal vigilance is the key-note to Tori's attitude. Tori must also learn to expel *kiai* with the correct spirit. When Tori executes a counterattack using *atemi-waza* with the feet or the hands, it is customary to use the *kiai* or verbal shout. The word *kiai* is made up of two syllables, *ki* and *ai*. *Ki* literally means a combination of 'psychic and physical energy summoned from within oneself', and *ai* is a contraction of the verb *awasu*, 'to unite'.*

Psychologically, it is the art of concentrating one mental's energy entirely on a single objective. Physically, it is the art of special breathing techniques which involve filling the *seika-tanden* or *haragei* (an area of the abdomen just below the navel), whilst executing the actual verbal shout, 'eitt', with an essentially aggressive intonation. The psychological and physical efforts are united and combined by *kime* (focus); the *kiai* is executed with integrated force. The end effect is that the attacker, Uke, has been startled, psyched out, and finally subdued by the overwhelming psychological and physical prowess of Tori.

When practising the role of Uke, one is required to have excellent attacking spirit and initiative. Uke should be skilful in the use of the *bokken* and dagger and should perform the traditional ritual of this kata with dignity and bearing. Uke must also practise the skills of attacking with the bare hands and performing the necessary *ukemi* or breakfalling.

To perform both sides of *Kime-no-kata* with excellence, both as Uke and Tori, requires many years of constant practice.

*E. J. Harrison, *Fighting Spirit of Japan*, 129–130
Secrets of the Samurai, Ratti & Westbrook, 370

Opening movements Both Uke and Tori stand facing the *joseki* or official platform at a distance of approximately four metres, two tatami or twelve feet apart. Tori is standing on the left side, facing the *joseki* and Uke on the right side. Uke is holding in the right hand the *bokken* and dagger. Both weapons are held with the curvature facing upwards, with the dagger on the inside of the *bokken*.

Both perform a standing bow to the *joseki* or official platform, then both turn and face each other. Both Uke and Tori kneel down by moving the left foot back and kneeling on the left knee, toes set, then going down on the right knee, then unsetting their toes and sitting perfectly upright in *seiza* position. Uke then places the *bokken*, with the *tsuba* or handle guard in line with the right knee, on to the tatami with the curvature inwards, then the dagger with the top of the handle in line with the *tsuba* or handle guard and the curvature also facing inwards. Uke then sits upright again. Both pause and calm their equilibrium, then both exchange a kneeling bow.

Uke picks up the dagger with the right hand and places it into the palm of the left hand, then picks up the *bokken* and places it also into the left hand. Then, taking a grip with the right hand completely over both weapons, Uke balances the weapons in the right hand, holding them by the right side. Uke stands up by raising

the right knee and simultaneously setting her toes, then the left knee, coming up to *shizentai* posture. Uke turns around one hundred and eighty degrees and walks forward approximately one tatami, two metres or six feet.

Uke kneels down on the left knee, toes set, then onto the right knee, then unsetting her toes, Uke sits completely upright in the kneeling posture.

Leaning forward, Uke places the *bokken* onto the tatami with the handle towards the *joseki*, then the dagger inside the *bokken*. Both weapons have the curvature facing inwards towards Uke.

As Uke begins to stand up, Tori also stands up. Uke turns in to face Tori and both move forward, commencing on the left foot, to a distance of one tatami.

Both kneel down onto their left knee, toes set, then onto their right knee and, unsetting their toes, both kneel in an upright dignified posture and pause briefly.

Uke and Tori simultaneously move closer to each other on their knees by extending their thumbs forward and moving the right knee forward, then drawing up the left knee, until they come to the centre.

Uke and Tori sit completely upright in *seiza* posture with their knees approximately one fist space apart.

Set One

1. *Ryote-dori* (Both Wrists Seizure)

1

Uke seizes both of Tori's wrists.

2

Tori pulls both wrists backwards and simultaneously setting her toes, Tori kicks with the ball of her right foot to the pit of Uke's stomach.

3

Returning the right knee into position, Tori opens the left knee ninety degrees leftwards and, breaking Uke's balance forward, Tori swings Uke's left arm forward.

4

Breaking the grip off her left wrist, Tori applies *Ude-hishigi-waki-gatame* to Uke's left elbow. Uke submits by tapping the tatami twice with the right hand.

2. *Tsukkake* (Stomach Punch)

1

Uke closes the right fist at belt level, then thrusts the right fist uppermost into the pit of Tori's stomach.

Tori executes a right body evasion movement by turning ninety degrees to the right, simultaneously setting the toes of her left foot and opening the right knee up. Tori seizes Uke's right elbow with the left hand and executes a blow directly between Uke's eyes with a right inverted fist.

Tori seizes Uke's right fist with her right hand and places it onto her right upper thigh firmly, while simultaneously wrapping the left arm around Uke's neck and seizing Uke's right upper lapel with the left hand (thumb inserted). Tori moves forward slightly while breathing out and presses her abdomen against Uke's right elbow joint, strongly applying *Hara-gatame* or Stomach Armlock. Uke submits by tapping the tatami with the left hand and Tori releases Uke immediately.

3. Suri-age (Thrust at the Forehead)

1

Uke raises herself upwards and attempts to hit Tori with a right open hand thrust to the upper forehead, in an attempt to dislocate Tori's neck backwards.

2

Tori raises herself up, setting her toes and immediately seizes Uke's right wrist with the right hand inverted grip, simultaneously gripping Uke's right armpit with a left inverted grip, while kicking Uke in the groin with the ball of the right foot.

3

Tori swings around ninety degrees to the right, placing her right knee onto the tatami and simultaneously breaking Uke's balance directly forward with a strong pull downwards with both hands.

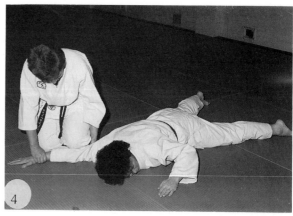

4

Tori moves Uke's right arm out to a position at right angles to Uke's body and advances her left knee one pace, then her right knee. Then, placing her left knee onto Uke's right elbow joint, Tori presses firmly down, causing Uke to submit with the left hand twice on the tatami. Tori releases Uke immediately.

4. *Yoko-uchi* (Blow at the Left Temple)

1

Uke raises herself up and attempts to hit Tori to the left temple with the little finger edge of the right hand.

2

Tori evades the blow by ducking under Uke's right armpit and encircling Uke's neck with the right arm, while simultaneously raising the right knee and setting the toes of her left foot. Tori presses firmly into Uke's lower back with the left hand, breaking Uke's balance to Uke's right back corner.

3

Tori pushes Uke down onto the tatami into a *Kata-gatame* position, controlling Uke's right arm with a left open hand grip.

4

Tori pushes Uke's right arm downwards firmly with the left hand while executing a severe blow to the pit of Uke's stomach with the point of the right elbow, emitting a sharp *kiai*, 'eitt'.

5. *Ushiro-dori* (Shoulder Seizure from Behind)

Uke stands up and walks around Tori's right side.

Uke kneels down on the left knee, then onto the right knee, taking a full kneeling position behind Tori.

Uke suddenly attacks Tori by raising the right knee and setting the toes of the left foot and putting both arms tightly around Tori's shoulders.

Tori raises herself upwards, setting her toes and straightening her right leg underneath Uke's legs and raising both arms upwards.

Tori seizes Uke's arm with both hands and drives the right leg back in between Uke's legs.

Tori pulls Uke in close contact on her back and pulling firmly on Uke's left arm, Tori rolls Uke over her left shoulder to the left front corner.

Tori turns to her right side, pinning Uke underneath her chest and bracing Uke's body with her right hand. Tori then turns her chest forward, taking advantage of the established momentum, and executes a blow with the left fist to Uke's testicles, or in the case of a woman, the hypogastrium, about one inch below the navel.

6. *Tsukkomi* (Dagger Thrust at the Stomach)

Uke stands up and walks around the right side of Tori, assuming a kneeling position approximately one tatami or two metres apart from Tori.

Uke then stands, turns around one hundred and eight degrees, walks back to the weapon position and kneels down. Uke bends forward and picks up the dagger with the right hand over the left.

Uke conceals the dagger inside her judogi and, taking both hands away, stands, turns in and faces Tori, and returns back to a position of approximately one metre or half a tatami from Tori.

Uke kneels down, then draws herself a little closer to Tori. Then, suddenly, Uke puts her right hand inside her judogi, holding the left hand over the top of her judogi, and begins to raise herself up in preparation for attack.

Uke raises the left knee up and thrusts the dagger (right hand) forward towards Tori's stomach. Tori executes a right ninety degree body evasion movement, bringing the right knee up, setting the toes of the left foot, seizing Uke's right elbow with the left hand and delivering a blow to the centre of Uke's eyes (*uto*), with a right inverted fist.

Tori seizes Uke's right wrist with the right hand and pulls it firmly onto the top of her right thigh, while encircling Uke's neck with the left arm (thumb inserted), and moving forward two small paces. Drawing Uke forward and simultaneously exhaling, Tori tightens the choke-lock with the right hand and presses against Uke's elbow joint with her abdomen applying *Hara-gatame* or Stomach Armlock. Uke submits by tapping her own left thigh twice. Tori releases Uke immediately.

7. *Kiri-komi* (Straight Cut-down at Head with a Dagger)

1

Uke sets the dagger into an imaginary scabbard on her left side. Uke raises herself up setting her toes and, pulling the dagger out with the right hand, executes a direct head cut.

2

Tori executes a right ninety degree body evasion movement, setting the toes of the left foot and seizing Uke's right wrist with both hands.

3

Tori draws Uke's right wrist towards her right shoulder firmly.

4

Tori then wraps her left elbow over Uke's right elbow joint and moving forward two small paces, Tori forces Uke to submit by tapping against her left thigh twice as Tori successfully applies *Waki-gatame*.

8. *Yoko-tsuki* (Side Thrust with a Dagger)

Uke conceals the dagger inside her judogi again and stands up, walking around the right side of Tori.

Uke kneels down next to Tori's right side.

Uke draws out the dagger in her right hand.

Uke lunges forward attempting to thrust the dagger (right hand) into Tori's right side. Uke brings the left knee up and sets the toes of the right foot. Tori executes a right ninety degree body evasion movement opening up her right knee, setting the toes of the left foot, seizing Uke's right elbow with the left hand and executing a blow with the right inverted fist in between Uke's eyes (*uto*).

Tori seizes Uke's right wrist with the right hand, pulling it onto her right upper thigh strongly and simultaneously encircling Uke's neck with the left hand (thumb inserted), seizing Uke's right upper lapel. Tori exhales, pushing her abdomen against Uke's right elbow joint and tightening the chokelock simultaneously.

Uke returns to a kneeling position approximately one tatami, two metres or six feet apart from Tori. Uke then stands up and turns around one hundred and eighty degrees to return to the weapon position. Uke then kneels down, replacing the dagger and adjusting her judogi. Both Uke and Tori stand, indicating the conclusion of the first set.

Set Two *Tachiai*

9. *Ryote-dori* (Both Wrists Seizure)

Uke attacks Tori by seizing both wrists.

Tori immediately pulls both wrists backwards, pulling Uke forward, and simultaneously executes a kick to Uke's testicles with the ball of the right foot.

Tori lowers the right foot again and swings Uke's left arm across, while breaking off Uke's right grip on her left wrist.

Tori draws Uke forward two small steps, wrapping her right arm over Uke's left elbow joint, applying *Waki-gatame*. Uke submits by tapping on Tori's right thigh.

10. *Sode-dori* (Sleeve Seizure from the Side)

Uke passes on Tori's right side, then behind Tori and pauses at Tori's left side. Uke seizes Tori's left outside judogi sleeve and begins to force Tori to walk forward.

Both move forward on the right foot, then on the left foot, but on the third step forward, just as Tori's right foot comes forward and to the right side, Tori executes a left side kick with the edge of the foot against Uke's right knee joint emitting a sharp *kiai* (*eitt*).

Tori places her left foot down onto the tatami and executes a one hundred and eighty degree turn, seizing Uke's judogi with both hands, breaking Uke's balance to her right back corner.

Tori executes a *migi* or right side *O-soto-gari* technique.

Uke is thrown directly backwards.

Both pause briefly after throwing, then Uke stands and walks back around Tori and both face each other at a distance of approximately two metres or one tatami for the next movement.

255

11. *Tsuki-kake* (Straight Strike to the Face)

Uke raises both fists uppermost, leading with the left foot and the left fist extended. Uke advances the left foot forward one pace in a feinting gesture, giving Tori the impression that she will strike with the left fist.

When Uke is within striking distance, she advances the right foot one big step forward bringing the right fist out in a surprise movement with the intention of striking Tori directly between the eyes (*uto*).

Tori executes a right ninety degree body movement, seizing Uke's right wrist and pulling downwards, breaking Uke's balance forward.

Tori steps quickly behind Uke, crossing her right foot over her left and seizes Uke's throat with the right forearm, clasping the right hand in the left. Tori presses the right side of her head against Uke's neck applying *Hadaka-jime* and breaking Uke's balance backwards.

12. *Tsuki-age* (Upper-cut)

Uke advances the right foot forward and brings the right fist up towards Tori's chin.

Tori moves her head back to avoid Uke's right fist and simultaneously executes a right ninety degree body evasion movement seizing Uke's right wrist with both hands.

Tori advances forward several small paces, while simultaneously wrapping her left elbow firmly over Uke's right elbow joint, stretching Uke's arm outwards, applying *Ude-hishigi-waki-gatame*.

13. *Suri-age* (Thrust at the Forehead)

Uke advances her right foot, attacking Tori with a right open hand thrust at Tori's forehead. Tori executes a left open hand block, while simultaneously executing a right blow to Uke's solar plexus.

Tori seizes Uke's left arm and makes an entry for *hidari* or left *Uki-goshi*.

Tori throws Uke directly forward.

Both pause briefly after throwing, then Uke stands and both face each other in *shizentai* posture for the next movement.

14. Yoko-uchi (Blow at the Left Temple)

Uke advances the right foot forward and attempts to execute a right inverted blow to Tori's left temple.

Tori advances the left foot forward, simultaneously ducking under Uke's right armpit, and inserting the right hand inside Uke's upper left lapel.

Tori advances the right foot to centre and passes the left arm over Uke's left shoulder, grasping Uke's right lapel applying *Okuri-eri-jime*.

15. *Keage* (Testicles Kick)

Uke attacks Tori with a right kick with the ball of the foot towards Tori's testicles.

Tori executes a right ninety degree body evasion movement, seizing Uke's right foot with both hands, the left hand grasping the heel and the right hand grasping the toes.

Tori executes a counter kick with the ball of the right foot, while pivoting forward on the left foot to face Uke again.

Uke walks around Tori on the right side in preparation for the next movement.

16. *Ushiro-dori* (Shoulder Seizure from Behind)

Uke and Tori walk forward together, commencing on the right foot.

Then on the left foot.

On the third step, just as their right foot is advancing, Uke attacks Tori from behind, wrapping both arms around Tori's shoulders.

Tori raises both arms and simultaneously sinks her body downwards, gripping Uke's right judogi sleeve with both hands and breaking Uke's balance to her right front corner.

Dropping onto the right knee, Tori throws Uke over her shoulder in *migi* or right side *Seoi-nage* or shoulder throw.

As Uke hits the tatami, Tori executes an open hand chop with the little finger edge of the right hand directly between Uke's eyes (*uto*) and gives a forceful *kiai* (*eitt*).

Both Uke and Tori stand and face each other in *shizentai*. Uke then turns away and walks back to the edge of the mat to the weapon position.

Uke kneels down on her left knee, then onto her right knee into *seiza* and selects the dagger. Crossing the right hand over the left, Uke picks up the dagger.

Uke then conceals the dagger inside her judogi and covers the left lapel over it. Uke stands up in *shizentai* posture, turns around one hundred and eighty degrees to face Tori again, and walks forward until approximately one metre or half a tatami from Tori.

17. *Tsuki-komi* (Dagger Thrust at the Stomach)

Uke attacks Tori with the dagger directly towards Tori's stomach, simultaneously advancing the left foot forward.

Tori executes a right ninety degree body evasion movement, seizing Uke's right elbow with the left hand and simultaneously executing a right inverted fist blow directly between Uke's eyes (*uto*).

Tori seizes Uke's right wrist with the right hand, placing it across her right thigh, and encircles Uke's neck with the left arm (thumb inserted). Tori seizes Uke's right lapel with the left hand, then advances the right foot forward.

Tori advances the left foot forward and, breathing out, pushes her abdomen out against Uke's right elbow joint, while exerting a chokelock against Uke's throat with the left hand. Tori applies *Hara-gatame* to the point of submission.

18. *Kiri-komi* (Straight Cut-down at Head with a Dagger)

Uke carries the dagger on the left hip in an imaginery scabbard, which is actually the left hand covering the dagger. Uke draws the dagger out, advancing the right foot forward, and makes a direct overhead cut with the right hand to the centre of Tori's head.

Tori executes a right ninety degree body evasion movement, moving the right leg backwards, and simultaneously seizes Uke's right wrist with both hands.

Tori pulls Uke's right elbow joint underneath her left armpit and simultaneously advances the right foot forward, then the left, drawing Uke towards the right front corner two small paces. Tori fully applies *Ude-hishigi-waki-gatame*.

Both Uke and Tori return to a position facing each other in *shizentai* posture. Uke holds the dagger in her right hand, by her right side. Uke turns away one hundred and eighty degrees and walks back to the weapon position. Kneeling down, she places the dagger back into position, crossing the right hand over the left. Uke sits upright and pauses briefly before commencing the next movement.

19. *Nuki-kake* (Sword Unsheathing)

Uke bends forward and picks up the *bokken*, crossing the right hand over the left.

Uke stands the *bokken* upright onto its tip, placing her right thumb onto the *tsuba* or handle guard.

Uke pulls her belt outwards on the left side, with her left thumb, simultaneously inserting the *bokken* into her belt.

After sliding the *bokken* completely into position, Uke takes the right hand away, then stands up in *shizentai* posture. Uke makes a one hundred and eighty degree turn around to face Tori.

Uke walks forward to approximately half a tatami or one metre in distance from Tori.

1

Uke suddenly tries to draw the *bokken* outwards. Tori immediately seizes Uke's right wrist with the right hand, restraining Uke's drawing out action, then advances the right foot forward.

2

Tori steps to the centre with the left foot whilst passing the left hand over Uke's left shoulder, seizing Uke's right lapel with the left hand.

3

Tori passes her right hand underneath Uke's right arm and swings Uke's right arm high in a circular motion, breaking Uke's balance backwards.

4

Tori places her right hand on the nape of Uke's neck and pulling Uke backwards, Tori applies *Kataha-jime* to Uke's neck to the point of submission. Uke taps the right foot in a signal of submission.

Tori releases Uke immediately and Uke adjusts her position to a distance of approximately nine feet apart, one and a half tatami or three metres.

20. *Kiri-oroshi* (Straight Cut-down with a Sword)

Uke advances the right foot, drawing out the *bokken* with the right hand, then balancing it in both hands, levelling it directly at the opponent's eyes. Uke then advances the right foot forward, drawing up the left, without moving the arms or the *bokken*. Tori adjusts to this feinting movement by moving backwards one pace on the right foot, then the left.

Uke then advances the right foot forward, bringing the *bokken* directly downwards towards the top of Tori's head. Tori executes a right ninety degree body evasion movement, moving the right leg back and simultaneously seizing Uke's right wrist with the right hand.

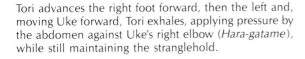

Tori advances the right foot forward, then the left and, moving Uke forward, Tori exhales, applying pressure by the abdomen against Uke's right elbow (*Hara-gatame*), while still maintaining the stranglehold.

Uke then suddenly advances the left foot forward half a pace, raising the *bokken* overhead with full force.

Tori pulls Uke's right wrist firmly onto the top of her own right thigh and passes her left arm around Uke's neck, seizing Uke's right collar (thumb inserted).

Uke withdraws the *bokken* with the right hand, pointing the tip of the *bokken* down towards the tatami and leaving the right foot forward. Uke levels the *bokken* at Tori's eye level, then proceeds to put the *bokken* into the left side of her belt.

Uke brings the right foot back into *shizentai* posture as the *bokken* is completely in. Uke turns around one hundred and eighty degrees and returns to the weapon position.

Uke kneels down and draws the *bokken* out of her left belt and places it back into position, crossing the right hand over the left. Uke pauses briefly then picks up the dagger first, then the *bokken* and, levelling them in the right hand, stands and turns in to face Tori.

Both step back on their right foot, then on their left foot into *shizentai* and adjust their distance to approximately twelve feet, two tatami or four metres. Then, closing their heels together, toes apart, both kneel down.

Uke lays out the *bokken* with the *tsuba* in line with her right knee, then the dagger with the handle in line with the *tsuba* or handle guard of the *bokken*.

Closing movements

Both Uke and Tori exchange a kneeling bow, then sit upright again. Uke places the dagger into the palm of the left hand, then the *bokken* next to it, then moves them into the right hand, with the dagger on the inside of the *bokken*, and the curvatures facing downwards. Both Uke and Tori stand up by raising the right knee, toes set, then the left. Both turn and face the *joseki* with their heels together and toes apart, then they perform a standing bow to the *joseki* in conclusion of *Kime-no-kata*.

Bodhidharma, Daruma Taishi, *Twenty-eighth Patriarch of Buddhism and Founder of Zen*
(*From a painting by Chodensu*)

The Mystique of the Martial Arts

The spriitual, esoteric, mysterious, yet awe-inspiring principles of the martial arts require many years to research and study and, in fact, a devoted practitioner can spend a lifetime doing just that.

An Indian Buddhist monk by the name of Bodhidharma, the Twenty-eighth Patriarch of Buddhism and the Founder of Zen (502–550 AD), had a profound influence on the esoteric teachings of the martial arts, by introducing the teachings of *Dharma*, Universal Law, or the Good Law.

It was Bodhidharma, whom the Japanese call Daruma Taishi and the Chinese call Tat Moh, who introduced *dhyana*, or silent meditation, into China, and when these teachings reached Japan in the seventh century AD they became known as Zen. Bodhidharma left India and travelled to China, where he taught a combination of callisthenics and yoga breathing techniques as a spiritual discipline, known as Kempo, in the Shaolin Monastery. This discipline was the forerunner of our modern day karate.

To understand the esoteric principles, one must begin by making a complete study, and the key to unlocking the enigma associated with the mystique of the martial arts is to study Buddhism. The occidental student of the martial arts is at a great disadvantage to begin with, because our basic religious and spiritual concepts are derived from the teachings of Christianity, which does not include these principles. To accept the esoteric teachings involved in the martial arts, one must be open minded enough to study comparative religion. To begin with, all of the secret doctrines of Buddhism, regardless of sect, teach the existence of an etheric counterpart to our physical body and, in fact, this etheric body has an electro-magnetic field commonly referred to as an *aura*.

The existence of our aura has recently been verified by high voltage photography, known as Kirlian photography.* Proof has been established that minerals, plants, animals and humans have an aura. The human aura has been depicted in the form of a golden halo in many religious paintings, seen around the heads of Saints and of our Christian Saviour, Jesus Christ, for many hundreds of years.

The etheric counterpart is composed of a dense physical matter, etheric in substance, faintly luminous and violet grey in colour, through which flow streams of vitality which keep the physical body alive. There are seven vital centres or *chakras*, which are wheel-like vortices, through which passes the central nerve channel, *sushumna*. The positive nerve channel, *pingala*, and the negative nerve channel, *ida*, cross over each other at the junctions which separate each *chakra*.

The Seven *Chakras*

Muladhara Chakra

The Muladhara chakra is located at the base of the spine. Its endocrine influence is the ovaries of the female and the gonads of the male. Its function is sex. The colours associated with this centre are the hot colours of red and orange. Symbolically, the square represents this centre. The branch of yoga associated with this centre is *Tantrik* yoga. The mantra or sound for this centre is *la*. The element belonging to this chakra is earth. The dominant faculty of this centre is the sense of smell. The negative emotions linked to this centre are frustration, rage and the positive emotion is passion. The related illnesses caused by the negative emotions are haemorrhoids, sciatica, prostate, ovaries, uterus. The planetary influence of this centre is Saturn.

Swadisthan Chakra

The location of this chakra is half-way between the pubis and the navel. Its function is our state of health. Its endocrine influence is the liver, pancreas and the spleen. The colour associated with this centre is pink. The symbolic shape of this chakra is a pyramid. The mantra, or sound for this centre is *ba*. The element of this chakra is water. The dominant faculty of this chakra is the sense of taste. The negative emotion connected with this centre is anxiety and the positive is well-being. The relative illnesses of this centre are diabetes and cancer. The planetary influence is Jupiter.

Manipura Chakra

The location of this chakra is the solar-plexus Its function is associated with power. The endocrine influence is the adrenal glands. The colour associated with this chakra is green. It is symbolically represented by a circle. The mantra or sound associated with this area is *ra*. The element is fire. The positive emotions connected with this chakra are desire, ambition, power and the negative are fear, guilt and doubt, which cause the related illnesses of ulcers and gall stones.

Anahata Chakra

The *Anahata chakra* is called the heart centre and is located in the centre of the chest. Its function is associated with compassion. The endocrine influence is the thymus gland. The colour connected with this chakra is golden yellow. Symbolically, it is represented by a cross. The mantra or sound for this chakra is *ym*. The element of this centre is air. The dominant faculty of this centre is the sense of touch. Venus is the planetary influence. The positive emotion associated with this chakra is joy and the negative is grief, which causes the related illnesses of angina, stroke and arthritis.

Vishuddha Chakra

This chakra is located in the middle of the throat and its function is that of creativity and self expression. The endocrine influence is the thyroid

Anatomy of the Etheric Counterpart
The Seven Vital Centres of Radiation

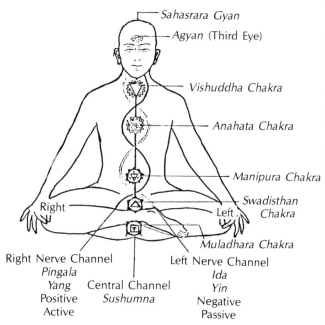

gland and the colour associated with this centre is sky blue. Symbolically, it is represented by a chalice shape. The mantra or sound is *ha*. The element is ether and the dominant associated faculty is hearing. The planetary influence is Mercury. The positive emotion associated with this centre is inspiration, whereas the negative emotion is repression, which is the cause of thyroid malfunction and the flu.

Agyan

The brow centre is located in the centre of the forehead. Its function is paranormal powers. The endocrine influence is the pituitary gland. The colour associated with this centre is indigo. Symbolically, it is represented by the six pointed star. The mantra or sound for this centre is *ah*. The planetary influences are the Sun and the Moon. The positive emotion associated with this centre is ecstasy, the negative is obsession, which causes schizophrenia and malfunction of the kidneys.

Sahasrara Gyan

This centre is known as the crown centre, because

it is located on the crown of the head. Its function is liberation. Its endocrine influence is the pineal gland. The associated colour is purple and, symbolically, it is represented by the lotus flower. The relative mantra or sound is *om*. The positive emotion of this centre is bliss and any negative emotion causes psychosis.

The symbol chosen to represent each chakra can vary according to the sect of Buddhism or the branch of yoga of the devotee.

Purpose and Function

Lying coiled up at the base of the lowest chakra, the *muladhara*, is a power or force known as *kundalini*, which is symbolically represented as a serpent. Through controlled breathing, known in Sanskrit as *pranayama*,[1] *kundalini* begins to gradually awaken. Having been aroused, the *kundalini* begins to rise upwards through the central nerve channel, *sushumna*, which corresponds to the spinal cord in the physical body, and pierces its way gradually through each junction at which *ida*, the negative nerve channel, and *pingala*, the positive nerve channel cross over each other and separate each chakra, according to Sanskrit terminology. As this force rises higher and higher, one's spiritual advancement increases. When *kundalini* is awakened in the lowest chakra one's sexual instincts are heightened, but extreme care must be taken to recognise this fact and exercise restraint in giving way to these physical urges, otherwise these forces will occupy one's consciousness continually. This is detrimental to spiritual advancement, mental and moral well-being and, in excess, will deplete one's nervous system, resulting, ultimately, in malfunction of the prostate, ovaries and uterus. However, when discipline is exercised, the sexual act, when perfected, is a profoundly blissful experience.[2]

As *kundalini* rises even higher and pierces through each chakra in turn correctly, one's spiritual advancement gradually increases and in combination with the correct breathing control and a physical discipline such as yoga *asanas*, or the martial arts, one's mental awareness increases and one's health improves enormously. When this force pierces the throat centre, one gradually becomes clairaudient, when it reaches the *agyan* or brow centre, one develops insight, or a Third Eye, and eventually becomes clairvoyant. If this force ever pierces the *Sahasrara Gyan*, one would reach a state of *Nirvana*, which is total enlightenment, at one with the consciousness of the entire Universe, the Godhead.

If one ever achieves *Nirvana*, one is said to be released from the Wheel of Life and the cycles of birth, death and constant rebirth.[3] One's soul is said to be liberated completely, and returns to the Godhead, becoming an integral part of the Universal Consciousness.[4]

If on the other hand, one falls victim to the many excesses in life, such as sex, alcohol, drugs, or whatever, one's soul is said to be eternally damned, and after death it would reside in a place where other fallen souls who can no longer redeem themselves dwell. See *Karma*, the law of moral retribution.

The etheric counterpart is a network of *nadi*, or etheric vessels, woven throughout the entire etheric counterpart like the threads of a spider web. These vast number of *nadi*, of varying sizes, which are sometimes parallel in their courses to the nerves and veins of the physical body, convey streams of polarised energy throughout the physical body, as well as the etheric counterpart, and cause the chakras to vibrate at certain vibratory rates. *Pranayama* means breathing control and when one becomes accustomed to breathing correctly, this stimulates the medula oblongata, which is the bulbous top of the spinal cord in the physical body. This regulates our breathing, which eventually pulsates at the correct rate to stimulate the pineal gland, via the fires or energies of the spine into the pituitary body and upwards into the pineal gland. This keeps the psychic forces, which pour through the individual, sublimated to the higher chakras. The vital currents which these psychic channels carry to nourish our bodies are fed to the physical organism through focal centres called the chakras.

In Sanskrit, the word *chakra* means 'wheel' or 'disc'. Many doctrines refer to the chakras as lotuses, because they resemble the lotus flower with a given number of petals. The chakras correspond to the endocrine system of the physical body. When the chakras are functioning harmoniously and vitalised energy from the Cosmos is flowing inwards and being utilised, our entire system becomes one with the Universe. However, if we abuse our physical body, for example by breathing foul polluted air, by smoking, or even by incorrect ways of breathing, by excessive use of drugs, by overeating, and many other harmful habits, then we create serious disturbances within the etheric counterpart and illnesses manifest in the physical body.

In Oriental medicine, the *nadi*, in their varying sizes, which run parallel in their courses to the nerves and veins of the physical body, are also aligned to the meridians in acupuncture, and the Chinese have made excellent use of these secret esoteric principles for thousands of years in curing a wide variety of common diseases. The Japanese also use *Shiatsu* and *Tsubo* therapy, which are based on the same principle of following the meridians, except that instead of using needles as in acupuncture, the Japanese use acupressure, applied with the thumbs and fingers.

It is vitally important to exercise constantly, eat correctly, rest regularly and stimulate one's mind, in order to inspire the best in oneself at all times. One must be aware of the constant planetary influences subtly affecting our minds and bodies also. The *manipura chakra* is aligned to the *haragi* or the *saika-tanden*, which is the sacred and mystical centre of the abdomen constantly being referred to in the martial arts as the area which, when controlled by breathing and centring of the consciousness, will produce a phenomenon known as *ki* in the Japanese language, or *chi* in the Chinese. The dominant faculty of the *manipura chakra* is sight, thus the meaning of *kime*, or focus. This word is derived from two syllables, *ki*, meaning psychic and physical energy united, and *me*, which means eyes in the Japanese language: thus, to focus one's energy through the eyes.

Many martial arts exponents can feel *ki*, and experience *kime*, but to do not understand the entire concept of its psychic and physical function. The *tamishiwaza*, or breaking techniques of karate, exemplify *ki* and *kime*. The karateka smashes through wood, cement blocks and bricks with apparent ease, without fully understanding how these principles work. Once again, care

should be taken to ensure against overuse or abuse of this energy force.

Kiai, or the verbal shout, is constantly used in the martial arts and this again is the use of the *manipura chakra* and certain mystical mantra or sounds, executed with psychic direction of the mind, as well as *pranayama* or breathing control, in conjunction with the contraction of the solar plexus centre at the moment of the verbal shout, 'eitt' or 'da-eitt'. The eyes are said to be the mirrors of the soul and at the moment of *kiai* can release enormous energy.

The philosophical and esoteric teachings are closely linked to martial arts and, in fact, become inseparable, because, in order to know why one must adopt a philosophical approach in judo and an impeccable reputation in one's private life as one becomes highly graded in the martial arts, one must be aware of the esoteric principles, research them thoroughly, and put them into daily practice.

Directly linked to the behavioural pattern in the martial arts is the Buddhist law of *karma*.[5] *Karma* is the law of moral retribution, whereby, not only does every cause have an effect, but, whoever puts the cause into action, suffers the effect. 'As ye sow, ye shall reap.' The pairs of opposites, good and evil, are very powerful forces indeed to contend with in our lives, and either one is attracted to good in many ways and will benefit one hundred fold, or one is attracted to evil, and will suffer one hundred fold. Therefore, the martial arts student is expected to make moderation the key note in all things. Buddhist followers study the eight-fold path, just as Christianity has the Ten Commandments.

People are judged on the company they keep, therefore one is expected to cultivate good and sincere friendships in life. One is expected to be prudent in speech, especially in the company of one's superiors. One is expected to respect one's superiors for their attainments in life and set an example of behaviour as a *Yudansha* when in the company of *mudansha* or students.

The energy channelled into one's mind and body has to be put to constructive use, otherwise it will become a destructive force. One must become creative and use the inspiration this energy creates, because, the more mental energy is used, the more healthy and powerful one's mind will become. The more physical energy is used, the more healthy and powerful the body will become. As *Yudansha*, it is vitally important to impress these facts upon the *mudansha* or students and encourage enthusiasm within each and every one.

If one is creative, one can benefit the Universe enormously. One can provide a wealth of knowledge for posterity and benefit the generations to come, as the originator of judo, Kano Shihan has done. One of the most famous mottos of Kano Shihan is 'Mutual Welfare and Benefit'.

In the various sects of Buddhism, one learns how to alter one's state of consciousness in meditation and in doing so, tap the higher consciousness of the Universe. Many devotees receive divine inspiration in doing so and ultimately become enlightened souls. There are many methods of meditation, but each method arrives at the same goal. Some devotees need to listen to certain mantra or sounds in conjunction with breathing exercises in order to induce a higher state of consciousness. It is a well documented fact that harsh sounds, such as disco music, busy traffic, city living, are all detrimental to spiritual advancement and are damaging to the physical body. Other sects stare in concentration at a mandala or visual pattern of a labyrinth in order to visually become transported, and enter the realm of higher states of consciousness via the eyes, ultimately trancending a state of tranquility and deep meditation. Other groups prefer absolute silence, as in Dhyana and Zen, in order to hear beyond the normal hearing range into a realm of inner hearing, sensing vibrations and sounds of nature, the very heart throb and pulsation of the Universe, and in doing so, attune their own bodies and souls to its rhythms therein and become one with the Universe.

[1] Sanskrit—ancient and sacred language of India.
[2] *Tantra. The Yoga of Sex*, Omar Garrison
[3] *Reincarnation*, Manly P. Hall
[4] *The Great Liberation*, Arthur Avalon
[5] *Karma and Rebirth*, Christmas Humphries

References

The Kirlian Aura, Gordon & Breach, Science Publishers Inc.
Energy, Ecstasy and Your Seven Vital Chakras, Bernard Gunther
The Complete Illustrated Book of Yoga, Swami Vishnudevananda
Tantra. The Yoga of Sex, Omar Garrison
The Story of Colour, Birren, Faber
Goethe's Theory of Colour, Maria Schindler
Encyclopedia of Esoteric Man, Benjamin Walker
Karma & Rebirth, Christmas Humphries
Reincarnation, Manly P. Hall
Subtle Body, David V. Transley
Secrets of the Samurai, Ratti & Westbrook
Esoteric Psychology 1 & 2, Alice A. Bailey
Tantra, the Principles of, Arthur Avalon
The Great Liberation, Arthur Avalon
The Serpent Power, Arthur Avalon
The Secret Teachings of all Ages, Manly P. Hall
The Tibetan Book of the Dead, Evan-Wentz
Astrology, Santha Rama Rau, Alan Leo, Isabelle Pagan
Asiatic Mythology, J. Hackin

Glossary

Acupuncture   Chinese needle therapy.
Agyan centre   Brow centre of the etheric counterpart.
Anahata centre   Heart centre of the etheric counterpart.
Ashi-harai   Foot or leg sweeping technique from the *ashi-waza* category.
Ashi-waza   Foot or leg technique category.
Aura   Health glow of the etheric counterpart.
Awase   To join or unite together.
Ayumi-ashi   Traditional walking in judo in which the feet proceed normally, one foot after the other, in a dignified, upright posture depicting body prowess.
Bodhidharma   Indian Buddhist monk, the Twenty-eighth Patriarch of Buddhism and the founder of Zen. Known in Japan as Daruma Taishi and in China as Tat Moh.
Dan   Grade in the Black Belt or Yudansha category.
De-ashi-harai   Advanced Foot Sweep.
Dharma   Universal Law or the Good law.
Dhyana   Silent meditation, introduced into China by Bodhidharma.
Dojo   Gymnasium or special hall for the practice of various martial arts.
Gokyo-no-waza   The five groups of throwing techniques which categorise the forty throws of judo, based on the principles of Kodokan Judo.
Goshin-ho   A pre-arranged formal self-defence kata, originated in 1946 by Jiro Nango, nephew of the originator of judo, Jigoro Kano, Shihan. (Women's Division).
Goshin-jitsu   A pre-arranged formal self-defence kata, formulated by the Kodokan Judo Institute in January, 1956.
Gyaku   Reverse position.
Happo-no-kuzushi   Eight directions of breaking the opponent's balance.
Hansoku-make   Violation of rules of competition judo.
Hane-goshi   Spring hip throw, from the *Koshi-waza* category.
Hane-makikomi   Spring hip sacrifice throw.
Harai   Sweeping action.
Harai-goshi   Sweeping loin throw, from the *Koshi-waza* category.
Harai-tsurikomi-ashi   Sweeping drawing ankle throw, from the *Ashi-waza* category.
Hidari   Left.
Hidari shizentai   Left fundamental natural posture.
Hidari jigotai   Left defence posture.
Hikiwake   Draw in judo contest. Both contestants receive a 'draw'.
Hiza-guruma   Knee wheel. A throw from the *Ashi-waza* category.
Ida   Negative nerve channel of the etheric counterpart representing the female force. *Yin* is the Chinese equivalent and Eve the symbolic Christian equivalent.

Ippon-seoi-nage   Shoulder throw, from the hand throwing or *Te-waza* category.
Jigotai   Defence posture.
Jikan   Term used to indicate 'time out' by the referee in a judo contest.
Joseki   Official platform of honour in the dojo.
Ju   Japanese ideogram connoting flexibility, suppleness of mind and body. More commonly translated as 'gentleness''.
Judo   The sport of judo derived from *Ju-jutsu* principles and techniques. Originated in 1882 by Jigoro Kano, Shihan as a system of training the mind and body in the best use of energy, a 'way' of life for the development of one's character.
Judogi   The traditional costume worn by all judo exponents.
Judoka   One who practises judo.
Ju-no-kata   A pre-arranged formal exercise called 'Forms of Gentleness'. Originated in 1887 by the founder of judo, Jigoro Kano, Shihan.
Kaeshi-waza   Counter techniques.
Kake   The actual moment of throwing, when a throwing technique is executed.
Kamiza   Seat of honour, which in a proper dojo is reserved for the highest graded Yudansha who have the most seniority.
Kangeiko   Special winter training programme of a vigorous nature, extended during the coldest days of the year.
Kansetsu-waza   Joint locking techniques.
Karma   Buddhist law of cause and effect and moral retribution, which determines the destiny of our lives.
Kata   Pre-arranged formal exercises which are performed with dignity and bearing and are highly ceremonial.
Katame-no-kata   A pre-arranged formal exercise of grappling techniques, originated by the founder of judo, Jigoro Kano, Shihan in 1887.
Katame-waza   General grappling techniques.
Keiko   Practice.
Kenshusei   Special squad selected for advanced preparation and training.
Kesa-gatame   A holding technique in judo called Scarf Hold.
Ki   A combination of psychic and physical energy.
Kiai   A verbal shout, executed in co-ordination with psychic and physical energy.
Kime   Concentrated focus of the eyes whilst executing psychic and physical energy.
Kodansha   A group of the highest graded, most senior members of the Kodokan Judo Institute, ranking from 5th dan and above.
Kodokan   The Kodokan Judo Institute in Tokyo, Japan, was founded in 1882 by the originator of Judo, Jigoro Kano, Shihan and is the world headquarters of Judo.
Koshiki-no-kata   A pre-arranged formal exercise

called 'Forms Antique'. The forms originated in the Kito school, one of the oldest *Ju-jutsu* schools in Japan, in which the late Kano Shihan studied *Ju-jutsu* in his youth.

Koshi-waza   Hip and loin throwing techniques.

Ko-soto-gake   Minor outer hooking technique from the *Ashi-waza* category.

Ko-soto-gari   Minor outer reaping technique from the *Ashi-waza* category.

Ko-uchi-gari   Minor inner reaping technique from the *Ashi-waza* category.

Kumi-kata   Method of gripping the opponent's jacket or judogi.

Kundalini   Symbolic serpent force lying coiled up in the lowest chakra of the etheric counterpart.

Kuzushi   To break the opponent's balance.

Kyu   Kyu grades are students who have not reached Black Belt degrees. Student grade or *mudansha*.

Maitta   A verbal shout indicating defeat. A judoka can also tap the tatami, or his or her own body, or the opponent's body twice, which indicates submission.

Makikomi   A winding action or technique which throws the opponent to the ground with the thrower also going down to the tatami, winding the opponent on his or her back.

Manipura   The solar-plexus chakra which is the sacred and mystical centre of the abdomen in the martial arts called the *haragi* or the *saika-tanden*.

Matte   Verbal command used in competition judo by the referee to indicate 'stop' or no further action permitted by the contestants.

Migi jigotai   Right defence posture.

Migi shizentai   Right fundamental natural posture.

Muladhara   Lowest chakra of the etheric counterpart.

Mudansha   A kyu grade student who has not reached the Black Belt degrees.

Nadi   Nerve current network of the etheric counterpart.

Nage-no-kata   A pre-arranged exercise depicting the various throwing principes or *waza*. There are fifteen techniques, which are executed to the left and right sides. This kata originated in 1887 and was created by the founder of judo, Jigoro Kano, Shihan.

Nage-waza   General throwing techniques.

Ne-waza   Techniques, both of throwing and grappling, performed on the knees, lying down and semi-lying down.

Nirvana   A state of spiritual enlightenment. Liberation.

Obi   Judo belt, which denotes the rank of the judo exponent.

Okuri-ashi-harai   Double ankle sweep. *Ashi-waza* category.

Osaekomi   A term used in judo contest by the referee to indicate a holding or immobilisation technique successfully applied.

Osaekomi toketa   A term used in judo contest by the referee to indicate that a holding technique successfully applied has now been broken.

O-soto-gari   Major outer reaping. A throwing technique of the *Ashi-waza* or foot and leg category.

O-uchi-gari   Major inner reaping technique from the foot or leg technique category.

Pingala   Right nerve channel of the etheric counterpart representing the male or positive force expressed in Sanskrit terminology. *Yang* is the Chinese equivalent and Adam is the Christian symbolic reference.

Randori   Literally means 'free exercise' in which both opponents are expected to experiment with their repertoire of throwing techniques, combination and counter techniques. Both are expected to display good attacking and evading spirit and try to catch each other off guard, at which time a throwing technique is applied.

Reigisaho   Dojo etiquette or 'mat manners'.

Renraku-waza   Combination techniques.

Renshi   Understudy to a sensei. Apprentice instructor or trainee, who can be from 1st dan to 3rd dan.

Renshu   Practice.

Renzoku-waza   Continuous technique.

Ritsurei   Formal standing bow.

Ryu   School or club.

Sahasrara Gyan   Crown centre of the etheric counterpart.

Sasae-tsurikomi-ashi   Propping drawing ankle throw from the *Ashi-waza* category.

Sanskrit   Ancient and sacred language of India.

Seiryoku-zenyo Kokumin-taiiku   A pre-arranged exercise called Forms of National Physical Education, based on the principle of Maximum Efficiency, which is one of the famous mottos of the founder of judo, Jigoro Kano, Shihan.

Seinen   Adult grade in judo, from seventeen years of age upwards.

Seiza   Kneeling seated posture used in formal dojo etiquette.

Sen   Initiative in applying mental power, technical skill and physical strength to gain advantage over the opponent.

Sensei   Teacher or instructor of the martial arts, from 4th dan upwards.

Sen-sen-no-sen   Highest form of initiative by which mental power, technical skill and physical strength are applied to gain advantage over the opponent before he or she can initiate an attack.

Seoi-nage   Shoulder throw. A technique from the *Te-waza* or hand throwing category.

Shiai   Contest judo. To fight to win.

Shiaijo   Contest area.

Shihan   Highest degree, tenth dan. The originator of judo, Jigoro Kano, Shihan, conferred a Doctorate of judo, twelfth dan upon himself.

Shime-waza   Choking or strangulation techniques.

Shimoseki   Lower seat or place in the dojo where students assemble.

Shiatsu   Acupressure or digital therapy.

Shizen-hontai   Basic fundamental natural posture.

Shochugeiko   Special summer training course of a vigorous nature conducted during the hottest days of the year.

Shonen Adolescent grade in judo, from fourteen to sixteen years of age.

Sotai renshu Practice with a partner.

Sukashi Evasive action, applied against the opponent's attack.

Sushumna Central nerve channel of the etheric counterpart.

Swadisthan chakra The second lowest chakra of the etheric counterpart.

Tachi waza Techniques applied in a standing posture.

Taiko Ceremonial drum used to call students to attention for the beginning of a training session or special lecture.

Tai-otoshi Body drop throw. A technique from the *Te-waza* or the hand throwing category.

Tai-sabaki Body turning movement.

Tandoku renshu Solo practice. To practise by oneself.

Tani-otoshi Valley drop. A throwing technique belonging to the *Yoko-sutemi* or side sacrifice category.

Tatami Traditional Japanese judo mats made from rice straw and used to practise various martial arts upon.

Te-waza Hand throwing category.

Tomoe-nage Stomach Throw. A throwing technique from the *Ma-sutemi-waza* or back sacrifice category.

Tori The partner who executes the throwing technique.

Tsubo Acupressure or digital therapy.

Tsugi-ashi A method of moving in which the forward foot advances and the rear foot is drawn up, or the reverse, the rear foot retreats and the front foot is drawn back.

Tsukuri To position one's body relative to the intended technique.

Tsurikomi A lift-pull action.

Tsurikomi-goshi Lift-pull loin throw. A throwing technique from the *Koshi-waza* or hip, loin category.

Uchikomi Repetitious entry for a throwing technique, without actually throwing.

Uchi-mata Inner Thigh Sweep. A throwing technique from the *Ashi-waza* category.

Uke The partner who makes a breakfall or *ukemi*.

Ukemi Method of breakfalling.

Ushiro-goshi Rear Hip Throw. A throwing technique from the *Koshi-waza* or hip, loin category.

Utsuri-goshi Changing Hip Throw. A throwing technique from the *Koshi-waza* or hip, loin category.

Vishuddha The throat centre of the etheric counterpart.

Waza Technique.

Wazari In contest judo, an award made by the referee to indicate a half point.

Yang In the Chinese language, the positive nerve channel of the etheric counterpart representing the male force.

Yin In the Chinese language, the negative nerve channel of the etheric counterpart representing the female force.

Yonen Pre-adolescent grade from ten to thirteen years of age.

Yudansha Black Belt Degree. These degrees commence at 1st dan, or *Shodan* and continue up to the tenth dan. The higher the dan grade, the more significant the degree.

Yudanshakai A federation or association of Black Belts which must be registered with the International Judo Federation and recognised by the Kodokan Judo Institute.

Yuseigachi In contest judo, a term used by the referee to award victory by superiority to the opponent who played better.

Zarei Formal bowing in a kneeling posture.

Zen Founded by Bodhidharma, the Twenty-eighth Patriarch of Buddhism, known in Japan as Daruma Taishi and in China as Tat Moh. An intricate religious philosophy involving the practice of silent meditation.

Zenpo-kaiten Forward rolling breakfall.

Zenpo-ukemi Forward rolling method of breakfalling.

Index

Japanese terms

English technical terms

General Index